Feasting on the Word®
WORSHIP COMPANION

ALSO AVAILABLE IN THIS SERIES

Feasting on the Word® Worship Companion:
Liturgies for Year C, Volume 1

Feasting on the Word® Worship Companion:
Liturgies for Year C, Volume 2

Feasting on the Word® Worship Companion:
Liturgies for Year A, Volume 1

Feasting on the Word® Worship Companion:
Liturgies for Year A, Volume 2

Feasting on the Word® Worship Companion:
Liturgies for Year B, Volume 1

Feasting on the Word®
WORSHIP COMPANION

❧ LITURGIES FOR YEAR B ❧
VOLUME 2

EDITED BY

Kimberly Bracken Long

WJK WESTMINSTER
JOHN KNOX PRESS
LOUISVILLE · KENTUCKY

© 2015 Westminster John Knox Press

First edition

Published by Westminster John Knox Press
Louisville, Kentucky

15 16 17 18 19 20 21 22 23 24—10 9 8 7 6 5 4 3 2 1

Scripture quotations from the New Revised Standard Version of the Bible are copyright © 1989 by the Division of Christian Education of the National Council of the Churches of Christ in the U.S.A. and are used by permission.

Permission is granted to churches to reprint individual prayers and liturgical texts for worship provided that the following notice is included: Reprinted by permission of Westminster John Knox Press from *Feasting on the Word® Worship Companion.* Copyright 2015.

Book design by Drew Stevens
Cover design by Lisa Buckley and Dilu Nicholas

Library of Congress Cataloging-in-Publication Data

Feasting on the Word worship companion : liturgies for Year C / edited by Kimberly Bracken Long. — 1st ed.
  p. cm.
  Includes index.
  ISBN 978-0-664-26038-5 (Year B, v. 6 alk. paper)
  ISBN 978-0-664-23804-9 (Year B, v. 5 alk. paper)
  ISBN 978-0-664-25962-4 (Year A, v. 4 alk. paper)
  ISBN 978-0-664-23803-2 (Year A, v. 3 alk. paper)
  ISBN 978-0-664-23918-3 (Year C, v. 2 alk. paper)
  ISBN 978-0-664-23805-6 (Year C, v. 1 alk. paper)
  1. Common lectionary (1992) 2. Lectionaries. 3. Worship programs.
  I. Long, Kimberly Bracken.
  BV199.L42F43 2012
  264'.13—dc23

                                                    2012011192

PRINTED IN THE UNITED STATES OF AMERICA

♾ The paper used in this publication meets the minimum requirements
of the American National Standard for Information Sciences—Permanence of Paper
for Printed Library Materials, ANSI Z39.48-1992.

Westminster John Knox Press advocates the responsible use of our natural resources. The text paper of this book is made from 30% post-consumer waste.

Contents

ix   INTRODUCTION

SEASON AFTER PENTECOST

1   Trinity Sunday

5   Proper 3 (Sunday between May 22 and May 28 inclusive)

10   Proper 4 (Sunday between May 29 and June 4 inclusive)
Semicontinuous   10
Complementary   14

21   Proper 5 (Sunday between June 5 and June 11 inclusive)
Semicontinuous   21
Complementary   25

31   Proper 6 (Sunday between June 12 and June 18)
Semicontinuous   31
Complementary   36

42   Proper 7 (Sunday between June 19 and June 25 inclusive)
Semicontinuous   42
Complementary   47

53   Proper 8 (Sunday between June 26 and July 2 inclusive)
Semicontinuous   53
Complementary   58

62   Proper 9 (Sunday between July 3 and July 9 inclusive)
Semicontinuous   62
Complementary   67

71   Proper 10 (Sunday between July 10 and July 16 inclusive)
Semicontinuous   71
Complementary   77

81   Proper 11 (Sunday between July 17 and July 23 inclusive)
Semicontinuous   81
Complementary   87

91   Proper 12 (Sunday between July 24 and July 30 inclusive)
Semicontinuous   91
Complementary   97

102   Proper 13 (Sunday between July 31 and August 6 inclusive)
Semicontinuous   102
Complementary   108

112   Proper 14 (Sunday between August 7 and August 13 inclusive)
Semicontinuous   112
Complementary   117

122   Proper 15 (Sunday between August 14 and August 20 inclusive)
Semicontinuous   122
Complementary   127

131   Proper 16 (Sunday between August 21 and August 27 inclusive)
Semicontinuous   131
Complementary   136

141   Proper 17 (Sunday between August 28 and September 3 inclusive)
Semicontinuous   141
Complementary   146

151   Proper 18 (Sunday between September 4 and September 10 inclusive)
Semicontinuous   151
Complementary   156

161   Proper 19 (Sunday between September 11 and September 17 inclusive)
      Semicontinuous   161
      Complementary   166

172   Proper 20 (Sunday between September 18 and September 24 inclusive)
      Semicontinuous   172
      Complementary   177

181   Proper 21 (Sunday between September 25 and October 1 inclusive)
      Semicontinuous   181
      Complementary   186

190   Proper 22 (Sunday between October 2 and October 8 inclusive)
      Semicontinuous   190
      Complementary   195

199   Proper 23 (Sunday between October 9 and October 15 inclusive)
      Semicontinuous   199
      Complementary   204

208   Proper 24 (Sunday between October 16 and October 22 inclusive)
      Semicontinuous   208
      Complementary   212

216   Proper 25 (Sunday between October 23 and October 29 inclusive)
      Semicontinuous   216
      Complementary   220

225   Proper 26 (Sunday between October 30 and November 5 inclusive)
      Semicontinuous   225
      Complementary   229

233   All Saints

238   Proper 27 (Sunday between November 6 and November 12 inclusive)
      Semicontinuous   238
      Complementary   242

246   Proper 28 (Sunday between November 13 and November 19 inclusive)
      Semicontinuous   246
      Complementary   250

254   Reign of Christ / Proper 29
        Semicontinuous   254
        Complementary   259

ADDITIONAL RESOURCES

265   Thanksgiving for Baptism
266   Great Prayers of Thanksgiving / Eucharistic Prayers
        General Use   266
        All Saints   269
        Reign of Christ   271

275   **SCRIPTURE INDEX**

Introduction

The *Feasting on the Word Worship Companion* offers language for the church's worship for every Sunday and holy day in the Revised Common Lectionary for Years A, B, and C. This volume provides liturgy for Year B, Trinity Sunday through Reign of Christ. It is intended to serve as a supplement to the liturgical resources of denominations and not as a substitute for any of those fine works.

The texts herein were written by people from six ecclesial bodies who share similar convictions about worship and its language, yet pray with distinct voices. As the writers come from a range of Protestant traditions, the attentive reader will notice some differences in theological background; in every case, however, it is our hope that these texts are grounded in deep and careful theological reflection. We seek to offer liturgy that is accessible yet elegant, in words that are poetic but not overwrought. These texts are written for the ear; we hope they are easily spoken, and their meanings quickly apprehended, in order to encourage full and rich congregational participation in the church's life of prayer.

These words are rooted in Scripture, as the church's liturgies have been for centuries. Using the Revised Common Lectionary as a guide, the writers of this volume offer words for worship that do not merely spring from their own imaginations but are grounded in the Word of God.

What This Book Includes

— Prayers and other liturgical texts—from Opening Words to Blessing— for every Sunday and holy day from Trinity Sunday through Reign of Christ (Year B)

— Thanksgiving for Baptism, for use at the beginning of a worship service or for reaffirmation of baptism
— Prayers for Communion, or Eucharist
— Questions for reflection on the texts for each Sunday and holy day
— Morning and evening prayers for household use, to be prayed by individuals, families, or groups, based on the week's lectionary readings. (These prayers are written in both singular and plural, so adapt them as needed.) These may be distributed throughout a congregation for use during the week as a way to continue reflecting on the Sunday texts.
— A CD-ROM, which enables worship planners to copy text and paste it in the worship bulletin. Permission is granted to reprint individual prayers and liturgical texts for worship provided that the following notice is included: Reprinted by permission of Westminster John Knox Press from *Feasting on the Word* Worship Companion. Copyright 2015.

Eucharistic prayers are provided in a separate section in acknowledgment that not all Christian churches celebrate the Lord's Supper every Sunday. In addition, one prayer for general use is provided along with prayers for All Saints and Reign of Christ.

How to Use This Book

One may use this book in a variety of ways. You may use the texts just as they are, or you may adapt them for your context. While new texts are offered for each Sunday, there is value in repeating portions of liturgy so that people might become familiar with them. When worshipers are able to speak the same set of words over a period of time, they are not continually adjusting to new ideas and patterns of speech. You may, for example, use the same prayer of confession for a season, allowing the people to enter more deeply into that prayer over time.

Although a basic fourfold pattern of worship is used here, the elements of worship may not be arranged in the same way they appear in your own church's order of worship. This is not intended to privilege one tradition over another, but simply to arrange the elements in a way that will look familiar to many who use this book.

You will notice that these texts are arranged in "sense lines"—that is, they look more like poems than paragraphs. This is intentional. The eye can pick up phrases quickly, enabling worshipers to pray them with greater understanding. So, if you reproduce any of these texts, please retain the sense lines.

This layout on the page also helps leaders to better speak the texts so that they can actually proclaim (and not just read) the texts, while maintaining eye contact with worshipers.

In cases where a congregational response is used, instructions are often included that will allow the prayers to be led without printing them in their entirety.

This book is full of words. Worship, however, does not happen on a page. As you use these texts, do not just read them. Pray them. Spend time with the words and make them your own so that you may lead with authenticity, wisdom, and a true sense of prayer.

A Word about the Lectionary

During Ordinary Time, or the season after Pentecost, liturgy is provided for both the semicontinuous and complementary streams of the Revised Common Lectionary. Each of these tracks uses the same Epistle and Gospel reading, but the Old Testament and Psalm lections are different. The semicontinuous track allows congregations to read continually through a book of Scripture from week to week. In the complementary track, the Old Testament readings are chosen to relate to (or complement) the Gospel reading of the day. In both cases, the psalm is understood as a response to the Old Testament reading. Liturgical resources for the Season after Pentecost appear in the second volume of each year in the lectionary cycle.

Since the numbering of Sundays after Pentecost varies from year to year, the designation of "Proper" is used here, as it is in the *Feasting on the Word* commentaries. It can be confusing to navigate the various ways churches designate Sundays; a handy resource for viewing all those labels in one place can be found at http://lectionary.library.vanderbilt.edu/, a user-friendly site provided to the public by Vanderbilt University.

Different Voices: The Ecumenical Nature of the Project

Each writer comes to his or her task having been formed by a particular liturgical tradition. We are Methodist, Episcopal, United Church of Christ, African American Episcopal, Presbyterian, and Lutheran, with a variety of backgrounds and experiences. Working as a team, we chose elements of worship that are common to all of us, as well as some elements that are particular to one church but not necessarily to another. Presbyterians, for instance, insist on including prayers of confession and prayers for illumination that invoke the Holy Spirit. Lutherans and Episcopalians expect a prayer for the day and include prayers for the departed in the intercessions. Lutherans also commonly use language about law and grace, and declarations of forgiveness sometimes refer to the ordination of the presider. These particularities were retained in order to preserve the ecumenical character of the book.

We use a variety of ways of praying but a consistent pattern of worship elements for each Sunday in the Christian year. Feel free to adapt the forms, change the words, or choose what is best suited for your context.

Who We Are

Just as this book is intended to serve as a companion to *Feasting on the Word: Preaching the Revised Common Lectionary,* we seek to be companions along the way with those of you who plan and lead worship.

The core team of writers includes:

Kimberly L. Clayton, Director of Contextual Education at Columbia Theological Seminary, Decatur, Georgia; Presbyterian Church (U.S.A.)

David Gambrell, Associate for Worship in the Office of Theology and Worship of the Presbyterian Church (U.S.A.), Louisville, Kentucky; Presbyterian Church (U.S.A.)

Daniel M. Geslin, Pastor of Union Congregational Church of Hancock, Hancock, Maine; United Church of Christ

Kimberly Bracken Long, Associate Professor of Worship, Columbia Theological Seminary, Decatur, Georgia; Presbyterian Church (U.S.A.)

L. Edward Phillips, Associate Professor of Worship and Liturgical Theology, Candler School of Theology, Atlanta, Georgia; United Methodist Church

Melinda Quivik, Liturgical Scholar, Houghton, Michigan; Evangelical Lutheran Church in America

Carol L. Wade, Dean of Christ Church Cathedral, Lexington, Kentucky; Episcopal Church

Other contributors include:

Marissa Galván-Valle, Louisville, Kentucky
Sharon Junn, Jackson, Tennessee
Yvonne J. Lembo, Philadelphia, Pennsylvania
Franklin E. Lewis, Chester, West Virginia
Martha Moore-Keish, Decatur, Georgia
Margaret LaMotte Torrence, Asheville, North Carolina
Cecilia Olusola Tribble, Nashville, Tennessee

The generosity of many people has helped bring this work to fruition. David Maxwell, executive editor of Westminster John Knox Press, has provided gentle guidance, shown great wisdom, and shared his seemingly boundless good humor. David Dobson, editorial director of WJK, has offered constant support and encouragement. Columbia Theological Seminary provided meeting space, hospitality, and encouragement for the project.

No words are sufficient to describe the depth of God's grace or beautiful enough to address to the creator of the cosmos. We offer these words with the prayer that they might be useful to the church in enabling worshiping communities to stammer forth their thanks and praise.

Kimberly Bracken Long

Trinity Sunday

Isaiah 6:1–8   Romans 8:12–17

Psalm 29   John 3:1–17

OPENING WORDS / CALL TO WORSHIP

Blessed be God, Eternal Majesty, Living Word,
   Abiding Spirit.
Glory to God forever. Amen.
Jesus said, the way to see God's dream for the world
is to be born from above by the Spirit. *John 3:3*
The way to take part in that dream, says Jesus,
is to be born of water and Spirit. *John 3:5*
That gift is available this day.
May you receive God's Spirit, be made whole,
and dwell more deeply in love divine. **Amen.**

CALL TO CONFESSION

Let us confess our sins to the One who gives life eternally.

PRAYER OF CONFESSION

Holy God, we know that you are always there to lead us,
yet we somehow lose our way and fall back into fear.
We confess that we have stumbled,
and we recognize our need for you to lift us up
and help us start again.
Forgive us our failings, restore us to strength,
and reconcile us with you, ourselves, and each other,
through the power of Christ and the gift of your Spirit. Amen.

DECLARATION OF FORGIVENESS

Sisters and brothers, hear the good news:
We did not receive the spirit of slavery, but rather
 the spirit of adoption. *Rom. 8:15*
Your guilt has departed; your sin is blotted out, *Isa. 6:7*
for you are God's beloved children—forgiven, loved,
 and free.
May God's peace be with you.
And also with you.

PRAYER OF THE DAY

Holy God, source of all goodness, you gave your Son
 for the life of the world
and sent your Spirit that your love might abide within us.
Teach us how to love each other this day,
that we may have life, and have it abundantly,
with you, in Christ, and through the Holy Spirit. **Amen.**

PRAYER FOR ILLUMINATION

Come, Holy Spirit, giver of life;
breathe into us that we may hear a word of truth this day.
Draw us into communion,
enable us to love,
conspire to make us one with you
for the world you so deeply love. **Amen.**

PRAYERS OF INTERCESSION

Let us offer our prayers, crying, Abba! Father! *Rom. 8:15–17*
knowing that it is God's Spirit bearing witness
 with our spirit,
that we are children and heirs of God.

Eternal God, we pray for the world,
that through the reconciling love of Christ
our destructive and violent ways may cease,
as you bless your human family with peace.

We pray for the mission of your church,
that empowered by your Spirit
we may proclaim the good news of the age
in the world you so dearly love.

We pray for all who suffer,
that together with Christ in his suffering
we may find healing as he did,
as he was raised and exalted in you.

We pray for your creation,
that as it groans for its redemption
we may care for its well-being
through the power of your life-giving Spirit.

We remember before you those who have died
and pray for those who will die today,
that through your glorious redemption that ends all suffering
they may rest with you eternally.

Through Christ, with Christ,
in the unity of the Holy Spirit,
we praise you, O God,
now and forever. **Amen.**

INVITATION TO THE OFFERING

For God so loved the world that he gave his only Son,
so that all who love him may have life eternally.
With loving hearts,
let us bring our offerings to God.

PRAYER OF THANKSGIVING/DEDICATION

**Holy God, your love overflows in the gift of your Spirit.
Bless these gifts that we offer
that they may spread your blessing
in a world of hurt and need;
in Christ's name. Amen.**

CHARGE

God said, "Whom shall I send, and who shall go for us?"
And Isaiah said, "Here am I; send me!"   *Isa. 6:8*
Life-giving God, free us from our fear,
fill us with your love, and send us forth in peace.

BLESSING

May the Lord give strength to the people.   *Ps. 29:11*
May the Lord bless the people with peace!
And the blessing of God, who creates, redeems, and restores,
be with you now and always.

Questions for Reflection

Jesus invites us to be born from above to receive new and abundant life.
Salvation, or abundant life, is understood as a present reality in the Gospel
of John. If the gift of God's love made known to us in Christ through the
Spirit is stirred up by gratitude, what daily practice could increase your
sense of gratitude? How could a simple practice of thanking God at any
given moment in the day enliven your experience of salvation?

Household Prayer: Morning

Life-giving God, awaken me to your threefold presence
in the world this day
that I may share your love with others
as freely as you have done for us in Christ. Amen.

Household Prayer: Evening

Abba, I give thanks for the immeasurable gifts of this day,
above all, for the gift of your love made known in Christ.
How grateful I am
that by his love I am counted as a precious member of your family.
Mere words cannot convey the wonder of this love. Amen.

Proper 3

(Sunday between May 22 and May 28 inclusive)

Hosea 2:14–20   2 Corinthians 3:1–6

Psalm 103:1–13, 22   Mark 2:13–22

OPENING WORDS / CALL TO WORSHIP

Bless the Lord, O my soul.   *Ps. 103:1*

And all that is within me, bless God's holy name.

PRAYER OF THE DAY

Holy One,   *Hos. 2:14; Ps. 103:13;*

we have no claim on you   *Mark 2:17; 2 Cor. 3:6*

except that you made us and will not let us go.

In this hour, suffer with your people once again

until we hear your voice in our wilderness

and remember whose we are;

for we pray in the name of the healer you sent,

and by your Spirit, which gives us life. **Amen.**

CALL TO CONFESSION

Jesus said,   *Mark 2:17*

those who are well have no need of a physician,
> but those who are sick.

I have come to call not the righteous, but sinners.

Assured of God's love, let us say how it is with us,

that we might hear more clearly the call of the Christ.

PRAYER OF CONFESSION

Gracious Creator,   *Mark 2:13–17*

we spend so much time hiding our fear, our anger,

our anxiety, our addictions;

we imagine ourselves invulnerable.

In your mercy, uncover our brokenness,

that we might be more truly known.

5

Holy Redeemer,
we have institutionalized our deceit;
we cater to the powerful and sequester the poor.
In your mercy, uncover our brokenness,
that we might be more truly known.

Sustaining Spirit, Great Physician,
you promise to receive us, wounded and welcomed,
    just as we are.
You bring life from ruptured offerings;
    you heal our disease.
In your mercy, mend our brokenness,
that *you* might be more truly known. Amen.

DECLARATION OF FORGIVENESS

Sisters and brothers,   *Ps. 103:8*
the Lord is merciful and gracious, slow to anger,
and abounding in steadfast love.
Believe this good news:
In Jesus Christ, our stories are known,
our sins are forgiven, our lives are made new.

PRAYER FOR ILLUMINATION

Spirit of the Living God,   *2 Cor. 3:2–3*
come now in power and write your word
    on our hearts.
Make us a letter of Christ to the world, a document
    of your grace,
for we pray in the name of Jesus, the Word
    made flesh. **Amen.**

PRAYERS OF INTERCESSION

Gracious Creator,   *Hos. 2:14–20;*
we were yours before we drew breath   *Mark 2:17–22*
and still we will be yours when the
    pulse of life ceases.
In every fragile, reckless moment, we belong to you.
We marvel at the ways that you give us to each other;
you bless us with bonds of kinship we have
    no right to claim.

And so we thank you for sisters and brothers
    who light the way for us,
who speak the truth in love,
who continue to hope even when we give them
    little reason to do so.
Holy God, may our gratitude for their steady presence
    make us quick to welcome,
to forgive, and to set more places at your table.

We pray for those who are losing hope because of
joblessness, or loneliness,
persistent pain, or powerful addiction.
We pray for soldiers who cannot rest and civilians
    who cannot heal.
Abolish war from the land; make your children
    lie down in safety.

Merciful God,
we pray that you would widen the circles of our concern.
Your ways are not our ways,
but you call us to be part of your peculiar family;
grant us the courage to be odd in a world so afraid
    of difference.
We pray for your children whom we label and
    keep at a distance:
the homeless, the alien, the terrorist, the felon—
    our categories are legion.

Redeeming God,
stake your claim on us now,
until we hear your gospel echo in each complicated story
and see your image shining from every broken face.
For we pray in the name of Jesus,
who unsettles our lives for the sake of your love. **Amen.**

INVITATION TO THE OFFERING
Sisters and brothers,
we cannot help but become like what we worship.
We bring our gifts this day as a sign
that we worship *not* what we hoard in our pockets,

but the one who is revealed in the act of self-giving.
Let us offer our lives in joy.

PRAYER OF THANKSGIVING/DEDICATION
Gracious God,
as we bring these offerings, we pray that our joy
    in the act of giving
might draw others to your table.
Use these gifts—have your way with us—
for we seek to follow Jesus, whose love is boundless.
Amen.

CHARGE
Beloved community, we are a letter of Christ,   *2 Cor. 3:2–3*
written not with ink, but with the Spirit
    of the living God.
May we be read and known
in our seeking after justice,
and in our offering of compassion
until the day of his return.

BLESSING
Now may the faithful love of the Creator,   *Hosea 2:20; Mark 2:17;*
the healing presence of the Christ,   *2 Cor. 3:6*
the life-giving power of the Spirit
attend you this day and forevermore.

Questions for Reflection

To what wilderness might God be calling you, in order that you might
know God's faithfulness more fully? Where might you be called to greater
vulnerability and deeper mutuality?

Household Prayer: Morning

Gracious, Holy God,
in this pregnant silence
open my heart to the miracle of your unwearied love,
that I might be this day a container of grace,
receiving the needs and gifts of others,
as you have welcomed me.

Use me as old, familiar cloak or supple wineskin, as you see fit,
for I would find my place in your purpose, and serve you as long as I live.
I pray in the name of the bridegroom, whose presence is joy. Amen.

Household Prayer: Evening

Gracious, Holy God,
as I remember the events of this day,
help me to see its encounters through the eyes of your love
that I might know you more fully
and receive this night in trust. Amen.

Proper 4

(Sunday between May 29 and June 4 inclusive)

SEMICONTINUOUS

1 Samuel 3:1–10 (11–20)   2 Corinthians 4:5–12
Psalm 139:1–6, 13–18   Mark 2:23–3:6

OPENING WORDS / CALL TO WORSHIP

We do not proclaim ourselves;   *2 Cor. 4:5–6*
we proclaim Jesus Christ as Lord
and ourselves as servants for Jesus' sake.
For God has shone in our hearts to give
knowledge of the glory of God.
Sisters and brothers, praise the Lord!
The Lord's name be praised!

CALL TO CONFESSION

Even before we speak, God knows our wrongs.   *Ps. 139:4*
Yet our repentance opens our hearts to God,
who is waiting to hear us and forgive us.
Let us confess all that separates us from God
  and others.

PRAYER OF CONFESSION

God who formed our inward parts and
  knows our hearts,   *Ps. 139:4, 13*
forgive us.
Instead of acknowledging you as our God,
we make our own idols.
Instead of proclaiming Jesus Christ as our Lord,   *2 Cor. 4:5*
we proclaim ourselves.
Instead of turning to the Holy Spirit,
we attempt to attain your way in our own
  understanding.   *Ps. 139:6*

10

Redirect our wrong ways
and lead us to the ways that make Jesus visible
   in our lives. Amen.   *2 Cor. 4:7*

DECLARATION OF FORGIVENESS
In Christ we died to our old selves and became
   new creations.   *2 Cor. 4:5, 11–12*
Therefore we proclaim Jesus Christ as our Lord,
and the life of Jesus is in us.
Thanks be to God.

PRAYER OF THE DAY
Lord God, who brings us mornings and beginnings,
touch our heart to hear your call today.
Grant us faith to rely on your extraordinary
   power in us   *2 Cor. 4:7, 11*
that the life of Jesus may be made visible
as we glorify you alone. **Amen.**

PRAYER FOR ILLUMINATION
May our hearts and minds be like the
   young boy Samuel   *1 Sam 3:7, 10*
who didn't know the Lord
yet earnestly waited to hear your word.
Speak to us, O Lord, through the power
   of the Holy Spirit,
for your servants are listening. **Amen.**

PRAYERS OF INTERCESSION
[A time of silence follows each petition.]
God of mercy,
we humbly ask that you hear us as
we lift up our prayers as a community of faith.

God of the Sabbath, who desires to give us rest:
hear the groaning of those to whom rest is unimaginable
because their safety is constantly threatened
and they are impoverished of their basic needs.

Hear the sound of those to whom
rest is a reality far away
because their hearts are broken with loss, grief, and pain
and their minds and body have grown weary
with illness and heavy burdens.

Stir us to heed your call as a church and as leaders,
as individuals, and as those who are in authority.
May we not be troubled by the mountains and the waves
of the struggles before us,
but may we trust in your extraordinary power.   *2 Cor. 4:7*

As we wait and press forward for the day
when rest is assured with justice, healing, and love,
grant us a peace that this world cannot give
but can be found only through Jesus Christ our Lord. **Amen**.

INVITATION TO THE OFFERING
If we take a moment to reflect where our
    rich blessings come from,
we know they are from the Lord.
Let us acknowledge God as the source of our blessings
through offering our gifts and ourselves.

PRAYER OF THANKSGIVING/DEDICATION
God of every harvest,
we offer our lives and the fruit of our labors to you   *2 Cor. 4:5–12*
that we may proclaim the life of Jesus Christ,
the true gift to all. **Amen.**

CHARGE
In a world filled with doubt,   *Mark 2:23–3:6*
that looks to the letter of the law,
go now as the letter of love
sharing the hope and the joy of life in Jesus Christ.   *2 Cor. 4:7–11*

BLESSING
May the love of our creator,   *Ps. 139:13–14*
the peace of the Lord of Sabbath,   *Deut. 5:14*
and the power of the Holy Spirit   *2 Cor. 4:6*
be upon you and shine through you.

Question for Reflection

Most of us strive to demonstrate trustworthy character in our lives, often not understanding trustworthy character as a fruit of our relationship with God. Reflect on 1 Samuel 3:19–20 ("As Samuel grew up, the LORD was with him and let none of his words fall to the ground. And all Israel from Dan to Beer-sheba knew that Samuel was a trustworthy prophet of the LORD"). How does this challenge our understanding of what makes us trustworthy?

Household Prayer: Morning

Praise the Lord, for it is your new mercy
that woke me this morning.
I praise you as I see your wonderful works through
    the window of day.
I praise you as I feel the movement of your
    mysterious works in me.
May this new day be a song to my Creator,
who is willing to befriend me in renewed grace. Amen.

Household Prayer: Evening

Lord, I close this day acknowledging you as my God,
my helper, my refuge, for it is your grace that sustained me all day.
I lay down my burdens of the unwise choices, the unfinished tasks;
I humbly ask that you may cover me in the blanket of mercy.
I praise you with a joyful song of your salvation
in which I find peace and hope through Jesus Christ. Amen.

Proper 4

(Sunday between May 29 and June 4 inclusive)

COMPLEMENTARY

Deuteronomy 5:12–15	2 Corinthians 4:5–12
Psalm 81:1–10	Mark 2:23–3:6

OPENING WORDS / CALL TO WORSHIP

Sing aloud to God our strength. *Ps. 81:1*
Shout for joy; raise a song!
With Miriam, we will sound the tambourine. *Ps. 81:2a*
From new moon to full moon, *Ps. 81:3, 6*
we praise the God who has freed our hands
from the brick baskets of Egypt.
With Moses, we praise God,
who feeds us with the finest of wheat *Ps. 81:16*
and with honey from the rock.
[or]
Observe the Sabbath day and keep it holy. *Deut. 5:12–15*
Six days we labor and do all our work—
but the seventh day is a Sabbath to the Lord our God.
Remember that you were a slave in the land of Egypt,
but God brought you out from there
with a mighty hand and an outstretched arm.
We, and the resident alien in our towns,
and all creatures great and small, rest;
giving thanks and praise to God,
who has set us free!

CALL TO CONFESSION

The hardness of our hearts grieves God. *Mark 3:6*
We prefer to follow our own counsel *Ps. 81:12–13*
rather than to seek and submit to the counsel of God.
Confessing our sin,
may God soften our hearts

and guide our feet
to walk in the ways of faithfulness.

PRAYER OF CONFESSION

    God of the outstretched arm,   *Deut. 5:15b*
    though you lead us into freedom,
    we choose again and again the chains of sin.
    Forgive us, we pray,
    for bowing to the false gods of our time: *Ps. 81:9*
    We believe we have made ourselves,
    rather than being made in your image—
    the work of your hands.
    We practice legalism against others,   *Mark 2:24*
    yet expect exceptions for ourselves.
    We rest in ease,   *Deut. 5:14*
    while others bear heavy burdens on our behalf.
    Heal us where we are withered   *Mark 3:5*
    in hand or heart or faith.
    Stretch us beyond what we have managed
        or imagined,
    to live as you intend and command.
    In the name of Christ, who came to
        set us free. Amen.   *Gal. 5:1*

DECLARATION OF FORGIVENESS

    We are clay jars with a treasure within—   *2 Cor. 4:7*
    an extraordinary power that does not come from us,
    but from God.
    We are not left crushed, despairing,   *2 Cor. 4:8–10, 12*
    forsaken, or destroyed.
    The life, death, and resurrection of Jesus Christ
    is visible and at work in us.
    Thanks be to God!

PRAYER OF THE DAY

    Gracious God,
    we thank you for giving the gift of Sabbath   *Deut. 5:12–14*
    in the midst of a busy and weary world.
    Help us to practice the Sabbath rhythm of life . . .
    work and rest, work and rest, work and rest.

We rest because you rested.
We rest because you command it.
We rest in order to remember
that the world and our worth
do not depend on our efforts and accomplishments.
We rest in such a way that others may also rest—
not only all other human beings,
but also creatures and creation itself.
You made the Sabbath for us
because you know all things
that are good and necessary for us.
We thank you;
we praise you;
we rest in you.
Gather us,
withered as we are,   *Mark 3:1–5*
in your mighty hand   *Deut. 5:15*
and outstretched arm. **Amen.**

PRAYER FOR ILLUMINATION

Shine in the darkness, O God,   *2 Cor. 4:5–6*
and shine in our hearts,
so that, by the power of your Holy Spirit,
we may grow in the knowledge of your glory,
proclaiming Jesus Christ and not ourselves,
until his life is made visible in us,   *2 Cor. 4:10, 11*
even in us. **Amen.**

PRAYERS OF INTERCESSION

Mighty God,
you lift the burdens from our shoulders   *Ps. 81:6*
and free our hands from oppression's weight.
We thank you for such power to save.
We pray for people who long and wait
for freedom and justice to come:
those trapped in the violence of war;
those struggling against unjust laws;
those weighed down by debt or long-term
    unemployment;
those bent low from hopelessness or grief.

Stretch out your arm, we pray,   *Deut. 5:15*
and set things right.
Bring us out from every form of slavery
into the abundant life you offer.

Healing God,   *Mark 3:5–6*
you know our illnesses and limitations;
our fears and secret pains;
our unclaimed gifts and discarded dreams.
So make us well, we ask, and set us free.
Give us courage to face our challenges
and to contend with past hurts.
Help us to see ourselves rightly,
putting to good use what you have entrusted to us
and daring to go in the direction of your voice and vision.

God of Sabbath rest,   *Deut. 5:12*
grant peace to your world wearied by work and worry;
depleted by environmental degradation;
beset by famine and fire and storm.
Renew the face of the earth, we pray.
Renew the faces of those
whose hollow eyes and swollen stomachs
call us to account for our casual wastefulness.
Renew the faces of those
who wander among us homeless or without legal status
while we lie down in ease.

Bring us to the day of your designing
when all things in heaven and on earth   *Col. 1:20*
will be reconciled,
and your great shalom shall fill all in all.
We ask this and all things in the name of Jesus Christ,
who is our hope. **Amen.**

INVITATION TO THE OFFERING
God lifts the burdens from our shoulders   *Ps. 81:6*
and frees our hands from work,
giving the gift of regular rest.   *Deut. 5:13*
What, then, shall we lift up to God in thanksgiving?

**In freedom and joy,
we give back to God a portion
of all we have received,
that others may rest in fullness of life.**

PRAYER OF THANKSGIVING/DEDICATION

For Sabbath rest, and finest wheat, and honey *Deut. 5:12-15;*
    from the rock, *Ps. 81:16*
and all other gifts that sustain us in life,
we thank you, O God.
Accept, we pray,
the gifts we offer in return;
our small hands reaching
toward your mighty hand, *Deut. 5:15b*
in gratitude and simple trust.
In Christ's name we pray. **Amen.**

CHARGE

Keep the Sabbath day holy *Deut. 5:12*
that all creation
may be healed and restored *Mark 2:23–3:6*
in the abundant life of God.

[or]

Remember the treasure within these clay jars, *2 Cor. 4:7, 10–11*
our mortal bodies,
an extraordinary power beyond our own:
the life of Jesus
that is being made visible in you.
Benediction
The grace of Christ surround you,
the Holy Spirit sustain you,
and the peace of God rest upon you,
now and always.

[or]

May the glory of God, *2 Cor. 4:6*
in the face of Christ,
shine upon you;
and the Holy Spirit make visible in you *2 Cor. 4:10–11*
the life, death, and resurrection of Jesus Christ
now and forever.

Questions for Reflection

In our 24/7 world where time is accounted for in mobile multifunctional devices, Sabbath rest is a countercultural concept and practice. What does Sabbath mean to you, and how do you practice it? What can you do to help make Sabbath rest possible for other people or for creation itself?

Household Prayer: Morning

The day, O God, began
when I awakened to receive it as a gift from you.
Help me this day to measure time well,
to see each moment within the larger sweep of time.
Whether I have time on my hands
or time slips through my fingers,
I have been given this very day
to live faithfully and well.
Help me, then, to touch the beauty of creation somewhere today
and remember that I am of the earth, too.
Help me to notice the face of Christ in some person today
and remember that we are brothers and sisters to one another.
Help me to hear your glory proclaimed in song or instrument today
until my own life hums with praise and thanksgiving.
I pray this in the name of Jesus Christ,
who is the same yesterday and today and forever. Amen.

Household Prayer: Evening

Your promised gift of rest comes to me now, dear God;
help me to receive it.
Give rest to all who wait this night
in illness or anxiety or sadness.
Let your rest come to animals that burrow in the ground,
to birds that nest in branches,
to creatures that swim in depths or shallows.
Give rest and renewal to all the earth.
To those who wander and work this night,
grant rest when the morning comes.
In Christ I pray. Amen.

[or]

God of extraordinary power,
remind me in these evening shadows
that though I am afflicted,
I am not crushed;
though perplexed,
I am not left to despair;
though I may have suffered wrong,
I am not forsaken;
and that even when I am struck down,
I am not destroyed;
because the life of Christ
is alive in me.
In his strong name,
and by his light, I pray. Amen.

Proper 5

(Sunday between June 5 and June 11 inclusive)

SEMICONTINUOUS

1 Samuel 8:4–11 (12–15),   2 Corinthians 4:13–5:1
16–20 (11:14–15)   Mark 3:20–35
Psalm 138

OPENING WORDS / CALL TO WORSHIP

O give thanks to the Lord with your whole heart.   *Ps. 138:1, 3, 8*
On the day I called, you answered me.
God's steadfast love endures forever.
Thanks be to God!

CALL TO CONFESSION

Let us confess our sins, for God has already forgiven us
and is calling us to return to the Lord.

PRAYER OF CONFESSION

Gracious God, have mercy on us,
for we have failed to be faithful to you,
though you have been faithful to us.
You show us your wisdom,
but we prefer to go our own way.
Our broken relationships with you and one another
have created poverty in us and our neighbors.
In your mercy, reconcile us to you and one another
for the work of justice, peace, and love,
through Jesus Christ, our redeemer. Amen.

DECLARATION OF FORGIVENESS

Sisters and brothers, do not lose heart.
When we call, God hears us; when we confess,
     God forgives us.
We believe and so we proclaim: In Jesus Christ,
     we are forgiven.   *2 Cor. 4:13*

21

PRAYER OF THE DAY

God of days,
we praise your name, for your grace sustains us.
We wait for you, Lord, for your word strengthens us.
Our outer nature is wasting away day by day,   *2 Cor. 4:16–5:1*
but our inner nature is being renewed by your
       daily bread.
Grant us the eyes to see what cannot be seen and to
       gaze on what is eternal.
May we revel in your work
and be a visible witness of your invisible kingdom.
In Jesus Christ we pray. **Amen.**

PRAYER FOR ILLUMINATION

Holy God, let your Spirit now move in us,
to turn us away from the temporary   *2 Cor. 4:13–5:1*
and move us to your eternal love
made visible in Jesus Christ, in whose name
       we pray. **Amen.**

PRAYERS OF INTERCESSION

Jesus says this is a house of prayer.
God, who is in the midst of us, hears us even before
       we say a word.
Thus God is waiting to hear from us and wants to
       work through our prayers.
As we pray, I invite you to name either aloud or silently
       particular places or people that enter your mind.
When I pray, "Come, come, O Holy Spirit,"
       respond with "hear our prayer."

O God in whose mercy we find refuge and strength,
we offer our petitions to you.
Guide us by your Spirit that our prayers may serve your will.

Hear our prayers of adoration and thanksgiving. . . .
[silence]
Come, come, O Holy Spirit,
hear our prayer.

Hear our prayers of longing for God's shalom. . . .
[silence]
Come, come, O Holy Spirit,
hear our prayer.

Hear our prayers of the needs of the community. . . .
[silence]
Come, come, O Holy Spirit,
hear our prayer.

Hear our prayers for interpersonal reconciliation. . . .
[silence]
Come, come, O Holy Spirit,
hear our prayer.

Hear our prayers for the world and for personal struggles
  with temptations and evil. . . .
[silence]
Come, come, O Holy Spirit,
hear our prayer.

All these things we pray in the name of Christ Jesus,
who points us to the saving grace
and the redeeming power in us. **Amen.**

INVITATION TO THE OFFERING
Let us continue to worship the Lord
through our gifts of talents, tithes, and ourselves.

PRAYER OF THANKSGIVING/DEDICATION
Eternal God,   *Mark 3:20–35;*
your son Jesus teaches us that a house divided   *2 Cor. 4:13–5:1*
  cannot stand.
Together, we offer ourselves and our gifts,
that they may be used to extend your grace to others
for your glory, through Jesus our Lord. **Amen.**

CHARGE
Our Lord Jesus says that whoever does the will of God   *Mark 3:35*
  is his kindred.
Go now and serve others as Jesus did.

BLESSING

> May the steadfast love of God give you hope, *Ps. 130:7;*
> the redeeming power of Christ give you courage, *Mark 3:35*
> the abiding presence of Spirit give you strength,
> as you serve the will of God
> this day and every day.

Question for Reflection

What unseen assurances of God's eternal glory are given to you this week?

Household Prayer: Morning

God of the morning,
awaken us to know that to be resurrected with Jesus
means to die with Christ first.
May we recognize you in every moment
so that whatever we do, we do for your glory,
through Jesus Christ, our way, truth, and life. Amen.

Household Prayer: Evening

God, all through this day you have
watched over me on the streets of my busy schedule,
nourished me with blessings that I cannot count.
And still your faithfulness does not sleep nor slumber,
but continues even when the sun goes down.
What a blessing to dwell in your presence!
In your presence, I lay down today's burden and take rest.
In your presence, may I rise to hear your voice. Amen.

Proper 5

(Sunday between June 5 and June 11 inclusive)

COMPLEMENTARY

Genesis 3:8–15   2 Corinthians 4:13–5:1
Psalm 130   Mark 3:20–35

OPENING WORDS / CALL TO WORSHIP

With God, there is: *Ps. 130*
Forgiveness.
Steadfast love.
Great power to redeem.
We wait for the Lord, who is our hope.
Through the long night,
we watch for God more passionately
than for the sun's first light!

CALL TO CONFESSION

If God kept track of sins,   *Ps. 130:3–4*
who would stand a chance?
But with God, there is forgiveness.
May God hear our request for mercy.

PRAYER OF CONFESSION

Merciful God,
we try to hide from your presence,   *Gen. 3:8–10*
knowing that we have traded your abundant life
for a wasteland of sin.
We have not followed your will,
but instead heed other voices
and pursue our own desires at the expense of others.
We are so misguided that we cannot discern
     good from evil,
making the wrong choice,
choosing the wrong side.

We ask for the courage to tell you truthfully
   what we have done.
We pray for forgiveness
so that we can live with ourselves,
with others,
and with you.
You alone can restore us.   *Ps. 130:7–8*
In steadfast love, look upon us
and reclothe us in your grace;
through Jesus Christ our Lord. Amen.

DECLARATION OF FORGIVENESS
Brothers and sisters,
do not lose heart.   *2 Cor. 4:15–16*
We are being renewed day by day
through the grace of Christ extended to us.
Thanks be to God!

PRAYER OF THE DAY
Once, dear God, we could hear you   *Gen. 3:8–9*
walking in the garden
at the time of the evening breeze.
Now, you call across the distance, "Where are you?"
And we echo back the same question,
   "Where are you?"
You wait and watch for us;   *Ps. 130:5–6*
we wait and watch for you.
Help us to see beyond the temporary to the eternal   *2 Cor. 4:16–18*
so that we do not lose heart.
Through the life, death, and resurrection
   of Jesus Christ,
help us to trust that our frailty
is received into your hospitable house in the heavens.   *2 Cor. 5:1*
Renew us day by day   *2 Cor. 4:16b–17*
until we come again into your presence,
where the weight of your glory
lifts us in grace and light.
In Christ, we pray. **Amen.**

PRAYER FOR ILLUMINATION

We are waiting, O God, to hear your Word, *Ps. 130:5*
for in your Word is our hope.
By the power of the Holy Spirit,
may we hear your voice *Ps. 130:2*
and be attentive to what you will say to us today.
In the name of Christ,
we ask this and all things. **Amen.**

PRAYERS OF INTERCESSION

God of Creation, *Gen. 1–3*
you set us in a verdant place
and gave us everything needful for an abundant life.
Yet we have marred your good creation.
We pray for the renewal of creation
as we seek to live more responsibly within it.
Make us better stewards than we have yet been
of water, soil, and air.
Teach us how to live
in ways that honor the habitats
of every living thing.

Loving God,
we have also marred human relationships
by emphasizing our differences and disagreements
at the expense of our commonalities and connections.
We pray that you will give us new understandings
and ways of living with one another:
doing the slow work of peace
rather than turning to the quick response of war;
receiving our various languages and colors as enrichments
rather than deficits;
caring for the least and the lost
not as unwanted burdens
but as welcome companions in your great household.

Renewing God,
we know so well that human life is fragile.
We see in our own bodies *2 Cor. 4:16–18*
how illnesses and infirmities afflict us.

Because you shared our human life,
we come before you to ask for healing, recovery,
and an end to pain and suffering.
Within our community, we remember before you
those in need of your care and ours. . . .
Within our own families and circles of friends,
we lift up the names of people in pain. . . .
We give thanks for the skills
of doctors and nurses and health care attendants.
We pray for researchers
who dedicate themselves to seeking new treatments
and cures and procedures
that enhance our health.
Strengthen all caregivers
with the gifts of kindness and patience and endurance.
We are grateful, O God, that though our bodies fail us,
you renew us spiritually day by day
so that we never outlive our usefulness to you.
No need, no person, is ever hidden from you
or beyond your reach to save.
Remember those we have overlooked,
those whom we have forgotten or forsaken,
and those who have wandered away from you.
Restore them, we pray, and restore us, too,
until we are all your family again.
In the name of Christ we pray. **Amen.**

INVITATION TO THE OFFERING

Who are Christ's brothers and sisters? *Mark 3:34–35*
Those who do the will of God.
Loving God, loving neighbor,
we share what we have
as members of the household of Christ.

PRAYER OF THANKSGIVING/DEDICATION

In the spirit of faith, Great God, *2 Cor. 4:13, 15*
we thank you for the opportunity
to give tithes and offerings,
to participate in extending your grace
to more and more people,
and to give all glory to you. **Amen.**

CHARGE

Do not lose heart,   *2 Cor. 4:16–17*
> for day by day
> we are being prepared for God's glory,
> immeasurable and eternal.

[*or*]

> Wait for the Lord;   *Ps. 130:5–7*
> hope in God,
> whose steadfast love endures forever.

BLESSING

> May our Creator, who seeks and finds us,   *Gen. 3:9*
> may Christ, who calls and claims us,   *Mark 3:35*
> and may the Holy Spirit, who renews us day by day, *2 Cor. 4:16*
> sustain us
> until all that is temporary   *2 Cor. 4:18*
> is gathered into God's eternal glory.

Questions for Reflection

As we age, we can see how our physical bodies do indeed suffer the wear and tear of life ("our outer nature is wasting away," as Paul puts it in 2 Cor. 4:16). Yet Paul says it is possible for our "inner nature" to be renewed every day. In your life, what contributes to your renewal? How are you being prepared "for an eternal weight of glory" (2 Cor. 4:16–18)?

Household Prayer: Morning

Morning has broken, loving God—the shards of light
scattering the long darkness of night.
Help me to carry into this day
the sure knowledge of your forgiveness,
steadfast love,
and great power to redeem.
May I do your will
in all my daily interactions
so that your grace extends
to more and more people.
I begin in thanksgiving,
your glory all around. Amen.

Household Prayer: Evening

Spirit of God,
come as the evening breeze,
carrying away the cares and little failings of this day.
Help me put to rest the worries I have,
the lists I keep,
the regrets I weigh.
You know me through and through—
I cannot hide from you.
May I lie down tonight covered
in your forgiveness and love and redemption,
and dream of things eternal.
I pray in Christ's name. Amen.

Proper 6

(Sunday between June 12 and June 18 inclusive)

SEMICONTINUOUS

1 Samuel 15:34–16:13	2 Corinthians 5:6–10
Psalm 20	(11–13), 14–17
	Mark 4:26–34

OPENING WORDS / CALL TO WORSHIP

The kingdom of God is like a mustard seed,   *Mark 4:31–32*
which is the smallest of seeds on earth;
it grows up and becomes the greatest of shrubs,
and the birds of the air make nests in its shade.
Give thanks to God, whose promised reign is coming.
Thanks be to God!

CALL TO CONFESSION

When we gather to worship God,   *2 Cor. 5:17*
we remember that we are God's people,
but we have often preferred our way instead of God's.
Trusting God's power to make us new persons in Christ,
let us confess our sin before God and one another.

PRAYER OF CONFESSION

Holy God, the parable of the mustard seed *2 Cor. 5:7;*
teaches us that a little faith can produce great work *Mark 4:26–34*
in your kingdom.
Yet we are too timid to bear the fruit of
  your righteousness,
for we walk by sight and not by faith.
Forgive us, Lord;
we do not uphold the poor or the oppressed.
We do not advocate for the powerless or the voiceless.
We do not sacrifice ourselves for the needs of
  our neighbors.

**Renew us with the love of Christ
so that we live no longer for ourselves,
but for Christ who became the seed of your
righteousness in us. Amen.**

DECLARATION OF FORGIVENESS

We who walk by faith and not by sight believe
  the good news—
If anyone is in Christ, there is a new creation:
everything old has passed away; see, everything
  has become new!
Praise be to God for the mercy and grace
that forgives our sins. Alleluia. Amen!

*2 Cor. 5:6–10,
14–17*

PRAYER OF THE DAY

God, you are the gardener of all creation.
You planted this world with the seeds of your love
and grow them with your faithfulness.
We are your harvest; we find our meaning and
  sustenance in you.
May our minds listen to you calling,
may our hearts be attuned to your will,
may our feet follow you in the world,
through Jesus, the Word become flesh. **Amen.**

PRAYER FOR ILLUMINATION

Holy Spirit, by your mysterious power
speak to us your truth and show us your wisdom,
that we may know you more deeply
and serve you more faithfully,
for the sake of Jesus Christ. **Amen.**

PRAYERS OF INTERCESSION

[A time of silence follows each petition.]
Lord our God,
who created all things
and promises us an eternal realm,
hear our prayers of intercession, spoken and unspoken.

Mark 4:26–34

We pray for peace.
[silence]
Eternal God, you sent us a Savior, Jesus Christ,
to break down the walls of hostility that divide us.
Send peace to the places where greed, pride, and anger
turn nation against nation, race against race, church
   against church.

We pray for the leaders of the church and the nations.
[silence]
Mighty God, sovereign over all,
give the leaders of the church and the leaders of nations
the vision of your kingdom, that they may lead us with
   justice and goodwill.

We pray for the earth, God's creation.
[silence]
God of creation, you made all things in your
   wisdom and love.
Grant us all a reverence for the earth
that we may use its resources rightly in the
   service of others
and to your honor and glory.

We pray for those who are in pain in body and mind.
[silence]
Merciful God, you bear the pain of the world.
Look with compassion on those who are sick.
Stand with those who sorrow.
Show them hope by your Word;
bring healing as a sign of your grace.

Let us pray for friends and families.
[silence]
God of love,
bless us and those we love, our friends and families,
so that by drawing close to you we may be drawn closer
   to each other.

All these things we ask in the name of Jesus Christ,
who died for us and rose for us,
who reminds us of your saving grace. **Amen.**

INVITATION TO THE OFFERING

God has provided us with all that we need.
It is our privilege to give back to God.
Let us return a portion of what God has so
freely given to us.
Let us now humbly bring our gifts to the Lord.

PRAYER OF THANKSGIVING/DEDICATION

Bless, O God, the gifts that we bring this day, *Mark 4:26–34*
that they may be a sign of our commitment to
your kingdom
and a pledge of our love for you and your world.
Multiply the work done by our time, treasures,
and talents,
that your presence and compassion may be known
in all the earth. **Amen.**

CHARGE

No longer regard yourselves or others from a
human point of view *2 Cor. 5:16–17*
but from God's view:
Everything old has passed away; see, everything
has become new!
Go forth from this place knowing that you are a
new creation in Christ Jesus.

BLESSING

May God grant you your heart's desire *Ps. 20:4*
and fulfill all your plans,
according to God's goodwill.

Question for Reflection

How can you practice walking by faith and not by sight?

Household Prayer: Morning

The sunlight greets me in morning,
reminding me that I begin this day in your presence.
The air I breathe instructs me that I live by your constant love.
Lord, I acknowledge you are my God!
I will seek your face in those I meet
and make my aim to please and serve you alone, Jesus, my Lord. Amen.

Household Prayer: Evening

The numerous stars shine the wonder of God
whose grace is beyond measure;
whisper to me your abundant grace, which sustains me.
As I lay down my head,
I recall Jesus saying that the Son of Man has no place to lay his head.
I imagine Jesus being with those who look for a place to lay their heads.
O God, I ask for your mercy
and pray for the day when we all can sleep in shalom,
trusting in your mysterious work through Jesus Christ,
the Savior for all. Amen.

Proper 6

(Sunday between June 12 and June 18 inclusive)

COMPLEMENTARY

Ezekiel 17:22–24	2 Corinthians 5:6–10
Psalm 92:1–4, 12–15	(11–13), 14–17
	Mark 4:26–34

OPENING WORDS / CALL TO WORSHIP

Small as a mustard seed and lofty as a cedar: *Mark 4:27, 31–32;*
The kingdom of God is growing.   *Ezek. 17:22–24b*
While we sleep and rise night and day:
The kingdom of God is growing.
The low are brought high; the high are brought low:
The kingdom of God is growing,
its large branches are home to all kinds of people!
[or]
It is good to give thanks to the Lord,   *Ps. 92:1–2*
to sing praise to God Most High;
to declare God's steadfast love in the morning
and God's faithfulness at nighttime.
Those who are planted in the house of the
    Lord flourish;   *Ps. 92:13–15*
no matter their age, they bear fruit
and remain lush and fresh, proclaiming:
The Lord is righteous! God is my rock!

CALL TO CONFESSION

God will not count our trespasses against us,   *2 Cor. 5:19–20*
longing instead for us to be reconciled.
We come before God, then,
in honesty, humility, and hope.

PRAYER OF CONFESSION

Gracious God,
we so often miss your kingdom at work among us.

36

Captivated by power and prestige,
we overlook the mustard seeds you have planted
 all around.   *Mark 4:31*
Forgive us for failing to notice
where and how you are at work.
Forgive us when we work against your plans
 and purposes—
fostering divisions when you have called us
 to a ministry of reconciliation;   *2 Cor. 5:18*
beset by apathy when the world has such deep needs;
building walls to keep people out when your branches
 offer generous nests.   *Mark 4:32*
Help us to grow in faithfulness, we pray,
so that we might reach our fullest height of faith.
In Christ's name we pray. Amen.

DECLARATION OF FORGIVENESS

If anyone is in Christ, there is a new creation: *2 Cor. 5:17–18, 20*
everything old has passed away;
see, everything has become new!
We are ambassadors for Christ,
for God has reconciled us through him!

PRAYER OF THE DAY

God, Sower of seeds,   *Mark 4:26*
be at work among us, we pray,
that your church may thrive in faithfulness.
Whether we are the size of a tall cedar   *Ezek. 17:22*
or are a small sprig,
it does not matter.
You are able to put us to good use.
Not by our efforts,   *Ezek. 17:22–23;*
but by your power and grace   *Mark 4:27*
we bear fruit,
produce boughs of spacious welcome.
You can make even a dry tree flourish!   *Ezek. 17:24c*
Even we can become a new creation!   *2 Cor. 5:17, 14*
Urge us on, then, in the love of Christ.
In his name we pray. **Amen.**

PRAYER FOR ILLUMINATION

Holy God,
we walk by faith and not by sight.   *2 Cor. 5:7*
So guide our steps in your Word today that,
by the power of the Holy Spirit,
we are kept from falling   *Jude 24*
and find our way in your way.
Through Christ, we pray. **Amen.**

PRAYERS OF INTERCESSION

God of all nations,   *Ezek. 17*
we thank you for your great power and might,
for you are moving all history
toward your good purposes and plans.
Though nations wield economic, political, and
    military power
that seems to rule the day,
we trust that you are stronger still.
We thank you that our systems of oppression and injustice
are ultimately doomed to failure.
We pray, then, for oppression to come to an end
and for injustice to cease,
so that people everywhere may live in peace and dignity.
We pray for all those who sit in the seats of power
to learn your ways of mercy and kindness.
In our community, teach us to work together
    for the common good,
caring for our neighbors
and growing in understanding across every divide.

Gracious God,
we know that you are at work
among the least, the lost, and the last,
in the things that are unseen,
and that your heavenly reign does not swagger,
    but is subtle—
coming among us in uncommon and often unnoticed ways.
Give us eyes to see and ears to hear
how and where you are moving and changing all things.

Help us to look for your kingdom in the ways of children
and others who are vulnerable among us,
to seek you at the margins among those overlooked
    or ostracized.
Humble us so that we can learn
from those who are meek in all the earth.

Life-giving God,
when our lives are dry and brittle,
we trust that you can restore us to life,
making us green again and fruitful.
For anyone living with depression,
chronic pain, or long-term illness,
we ask for your healing and tender care.
For those who have lost employment
or the opportunity to be engaged with others
    in meaningful service,
we pray for new opportunities to spring up.
For anyone who has come to an ending,
whether sought or undesired,
we pray that a new beginning will open
that promotes new growth and flourishing.
Finally, dear God,
no matter how small our faith is,
we pray that you will give us good growth
in our discipleship to you
so that we may be faithful ambassadors of Christ,   *2 Cor. 5:18, 20*
sharing his love
and working for the reconciliation of the world.
In Christ's name we pray. **Amen.**

INVITATION TO THE OFFERING
We give thanks in word and song to God,   *Ps. 92:1–4*
who makes us glad and gives us joy
because of all that God has done.
We enact our thanksgiving
through these tithes and offerings.
May God put to good use
what we give today.

PRAYER OF THANKSGIVING/DEDICATION

Life-giving God,
we know that you will accomplish everything
    you purpose.   *Ezek. 17:24c, d*
Accept, we pray, these offerings from our hands.
May they contribute to what you are doing
so that life may flourish.
In Jesus' name we pray. **Amen.**

CHARGE

Sleep and rise   *Mark 4:24, 32*
night and day
and keep alert
to the kingdom of God
all around.
[or]
Be reconciled to God through Christ   *2 Cor. 5:18–20*
and join in the ministry of reconciliation,
for the sake of the world.

BLESSING

May God bless you with new life,
Christ tend you in grace,
and the Holy Spirit guide your steps,
as you walk by faith   *2 Cor. 5:7*
now and forever.

Question for Reflection

The passage from 2 Corinthians urges us to be reconciled, to engage in the
ministry of reconciliation, and to be ambassadors for Christ. How can you
join in a ministry of reconciliation as an ambassador of Christ?

Household Prayer: Morning

New every morning are your mercies, Lord.
And new also is this day,
full of promise and possibility.
Give me eyes to see your new creation that is already
    coming into being,

even as I come and go among familiar places.
I pray that you will help me to see others
not from a human point of view,
but to see them through your eyes
of love, grace, and second chances.
I will try to walk by faith and not by sight alone.
And I will look for ways that I can be a part
of Christ's ministry of reconciliation.
In Jesus' name I pray. Amen.

Household Prayer: Evening

Gracious God,
with the psalmist I say:
It is good to declare your steadfast love in the morning
and your faithfulness by night.
For all the ways you loved me through the day that is past,
I give you thanks.
For your faithful watching over me tonight,
I also give thanks.
Like a bird asleep in its nest,
secure on a sturdy branch,
I—and all the world—rest in your wide embrace.
Despite all evidence to the contrary,
headlined in the news of this day,
I trust that your kingdom is growing;
that all of us are becoming a new creation
through the grace of Jesus Christ. Amen.

Proper 7

(Sunday between June 19 and June 25 inclusive)

SEMICONTINUOUS

1 Samuel 7:(1a, 4–11, 19–23) 32–49   2 Corinthians 6:1–13
    or 1 Samuel 17:57–18:5, 10–16   Mark 4:35–41
Psalm 9:9–20 *or* Psalm 133

OPENING WORDS / CALL TO WORSHIP

How very good and pleasant it is   *Ps. 133*
when sisters and brothers live together in unity!
It is like the precious oil on the head,
like the dew that falls on the mountains of Zion.
Together, let us worship God.

CALL TO CONFESSION

We strive to be strong and self-sufficient,
but in truth we are in constant need of grace.
In penitence and faith,
let us confess our weakness to God and to one another.

PRAYER OF CONFESSION

Most merciful God, forgive us.
We imagine that we can live without you,
when you give us our very breath.
We seek control over others
rather than strive to live in unity.
We allow fear to overtake us,   *Mark 4:35–41*
even though our lives are in your hands.
Draw us back into your steadfast love
and shape us into the likeness of your Son,
Jesus Christ, in whose name we pray. Amen.

DECLARATION OF FORGIVENESS

[Water is poured into the font.]
Sisters and brothers, the good news is this:
grace is poured out like water;
mercy flows like a never-ending stream,
bathing us in goodness and love.
Live, then, as those who have received new life,
rejoicing in your baptism.

PRAYER OF THE DAY

Holy God, you created the world and all that is in it.
The wind and the sea obey your Son. *Mark 4:41*
You are the source of our strength *1 Sam. 17:37*
and our confidence is in you.
All praise be to you,
our stronghold and savior. **Amen.** *Ps. 9:9*

PRAYER FOR ILLUMINATION

God of eternity,
by the power of your Spirit,
speak your Word to us this day,
that hearing, we may know your truth
and live ever more faithfully for you.
In Jesus' name we pray. **Amen.**

PRAYERS OF INTERCESSION

Let us bring our concerns for the world and for
    one another to God, praying,
Saving God, hear our prayer.

God of the sky and sea,
your world brims with glory.
You have set us in the midst of a garden
and trusted its tending to us.
We pray for our good Earth
and the wisdom to care for it well,
that generations to come may enjoy its fruits
and revel in its beauty.
Saving God, **hear our prayer.**

God of the earthquake and the storm,
your world is full of danger.
Keep watch over your people
and save them from despair;
strengthen and uphold them when trouble comes.
Saving God, **hear our prayer.**

God of power and might,
the rulers of this world do not always seek your wisdom.
Guide all nations in the ways of peace
and uphold the oppressed,
even as we work and wait for your coming realm.
Saving God, **hear our prayer.**

God of healing and comfort,
pain and loss are all around.
Soothe the frantic, embolden the fearful,
ease the suffering of the sick.
Give peace to all who grieve
and hope to those facing death.
Saving God, **hear our prayer.**

All-knowing, all-loving God,
we cannot always voice our hidden cares.
Hear our silent prayers, even those without words.
[A time of silence is kept.]
Saving God, **hear our prayer.**

With trust in your sustaining Spirit,
thanksgiving for your Son's interceding,
and confidence in your coming realm of justice,
    peace, and love,
we offer these prayers in the name of Jesus Christ,
    our Lord. **Amen.**

INVITATION TO THE OFFERING
With tithes and offerings give thanks to the Lord;
God's steadfast love endures forever.   *Ps. 107:1*

PRAYER OF THANKSGIVING/DEDICATION

We return to you, O God,
the gifts you have given,
that this money, and our lives,
might bear witness to the good news of Jesus Christ,
in whose name we pray. **Amen.**

CHARGE

Go out to be Christ's hands and feet,
and do not be afraid.

BLESSING

The creator of all that is
upholds your life;
Christ himself walks by your side;
the Spirit gives you breath
to speak God's grace
and sing God's praise.

Questions for Reflection

When do you let fear overtake you? How might you relinquish that fear
and trust in Jesus Christ?

Household Prayer: Morning

Whether I wake to birdsong or sirens
or the deep silence before dawn,
I awake to your presence,
most gracious God.
Enable me to trust completely in you
as I meet the challenges of this new day.
Make me watchful for your grace at work;
may all I do be a testament to your glory.
In Jesus' name I pray. Amen.

As I give myself over to sleep, dear Lord,
I thank you for the gift of rest.
Let me relinquish the cares of the day.
Forgive the ways I have failed you.
Restore me to you and renew my faithfulness,
that I may awake to serve you more,
for Jesus' sake. Amen.

Proper 7

(Sunday between June 19 and June 25 inclusive)

COMPLEMENTARY

Job 38:1–11   2 Corinthians 6:1–13
Psalm 107:1–3, 23–32   Mark 4:35–41

OPENING WORDS / CALL TO WORSHIP

God alone laid the foundations of the earth.   *Job 38:4*
The morning stars sang together   *Job 38:7*
and all the heavenly beings shouted for joy.
From the midst of the whirlwind, God speaks
   with power.   *Job 38:1*
We have seen the deeds of the Lord,   *Ps. 107:24–25, 29*
who commands and raises the stormy wind
and also makes the storm be still.
We ourselves have seen the wondrous deeds
   of the Lord!

CALL TO CONFESSION

Do not accept the grace of God in vain,   *2 Cor. 6:1–2*
for God has said:
At an acceptable time I have listened to you,
and on a day of salvation I have helped you.
Let us confess our sins before God,
who will listen and help us in our weakness.

PRAYER OF CONFESSION

Saving God,   *Mark 4:35–41*
we confess that our faith is too small,
our fear is too great.
When we are overwhelmed,
we think you do not care enough for us.
When life is uncertain and risky,
we are not sure we can trust you with our whole hearts.

Even when you move among us in powerful ways,
we question who you are.
Forgive us and calm our fears, we pray.
Teach us to trust in your power to save
and guide us in every circumstance.
Grant us your peace,   *Phil. 4:7*
which is clearly beyond our understanding.
In Christ's name we pray. Amen.

DECLARATION OF FORGIVENESS

Christ offers peace to our troubled souls.
Believe this One whom even the wind and the sea obey.   *Mark 4:41*
In Jesus Christ, we are forgiven!

PRAYER OF THE DAY

O Lord our God,
when we cry out to you in distress,   *Ps. 107:28–31*
you bring us through desperate circumstances.   *(Common*
You can quiet the storm to a whisper   *English Bible)*
and hush the sea's waves,
so great is your power.
Help us to trust you, then,
whatever we may face,
knowing that you will lead us
to the harbor we have been hoping for.
We offer you our thanks and praise. **Amen.**

PRAYER FOR ILLUMINATION

Holy God,
we know that our own words lack knowledge   *Job 38:2*
whenever we try to speak of you
or to you.
Yet we are drawn into your presence
and desire to understand all your mysteries.
So now, by the gift of your Holy Spirit,
speak your words and we will listen carefully,
responding in awe and gratitude.
Through Jesus Christ we pray. **Amen.**

PRAYERS OF INTERCESSION

God of power and might,
we come before you trembling with awe
for all you have done, are doing, and will do
in the grand sweep of time,
in the vast swath of creation.
Wield your power, we pray,
against all forces of nature
that threaten people, homes, and land
with danger and destruction.
Strengthen us for the work of rebuilding
wherever devastation has visited your people
through the work of nature's rhythms.
Speak words of comfort and hope
to those who have lost much,
or everything,
and must begin again.
We trust that your will for all people
is life and health and peace.

Wield your power, we pray,
against the forces of destruction we have devised
and are too quick to use against one another.
Dismantle in us the desire for war
until we dismantle our missiles and bombs.
Open our hands to embrace each other
until we cannot close our hands again
around the triggers of guns
or the timers for bombs.
Give us new tunes for that ancient poetry
until we all sing
of beating our swords into plowshares,
our spears into pruning hooks.
Bring the day, please God,
when there will be no more war of nation against nation.

Wield your power, too,
against the forces of illness and pain
that overtake our bodies, our minds, our spirits.
Empower us to fight against our addictions.

Job 38

Isa. 2:4

Help our bodies and minds overcome the diseases
that threaten our well-being.
Ease suffering; bring relief and rest to the weary
and comfort to the dying.
Wield your power over death,
our last enemy.
Give us courage and hope to trust in your gift
of resurrection and new life,
the harbor we were hoping for.   *Ps. 107:30b*

For the miracles of creation,
the miracles of birth, love shared,
a chance to begin again, reconciliation,
and the miracle of faith,
we give you our thanks and praise.
We are humbled that you love us
and draw near to us,
God of power and might.
In the name of Christ our Savior. **Amen.**

INVITATION TO THE OFFERING

We are invited, even urged, to open our hearts wide   *2 Cor. 6:11–12*
and to place no boundaries on our affection
     for God's people.
Let us then share generously our provisions
     with others.

PRAYER OF THANKSGIVING/DEDICATION

How grateful we are, O God,
that you call us to serve with the Holy Spirit,
who fills us with patience and generosity
     and genuine love.   *2 Cor. 6:6*
We pray that all we return to you
will be used faithfully
in ministry to the world.
In the name of Christ, we ask it. **Amen.**

CHARGE

In every circumstance,
trust in God,
who has great power
to save and keep us.

BLESSING

May the power of God uphold you,
the peace of Christ rest upon you,
and the Holy Spirit defend you,
now and always.

Questions for Reflection

Mark 4:35–41 tells of a time when the disciples were in great fear in a storm. Can you remember a time when you were in a frightening storm (literal or figurative) and felt in danger of being "swamped"? Did God feel far away or near to help you?

Household Prayer: Morning

Did you hear, O God,
the morning stars sing together this morning—
just as you heard them at the dawn of creation?
Open my ears today to the music of creation:
where it sings and rejoices,
where it groans in travail,
where it waits in silent longing.
Though I am very small
in the grand scheme of your design,
teach me to tend the earth in ways that increase joy;
to mend the earth in ways that restore fruitfulness;
and to wait with the earth for the hope of redemption;
in the name of Christ, my Savior. Amen.

Household Prayer: Evening

Loving God,
in your earthly life,
when evening had come
you led your disciples away
from the crowds and the busyness of the day.
You were so tired,
you fell asleep in the boat . . .
so tired that even a storm did not wake you up!
You know our weariness well,
our need to rest and sleep soundly.
Help me too, then, to leave behind
this crowded day,
my crowded thoughts.
Speak to me the words you spoke
to the wind and the waves:
Peace! Be still!
And, in faith, I will try to let go
of all that has been today and rest,
trusting in you.
In Jesus' name I pray. Amen.

Proper 8

(Sunday between June 26 and July 2 inclusive)

SEMICONTINUOUS

2 Samuel 1:1, 17–27   2 Corinthians 8:7–15
Psalm 130   Mark 5:21–43

OPENING WORDS / CALL TO WORSHIP

I wait for the Lord,   *Ps. 130:5–6*
my soul waits, and in God's word I hope.
My soul waits for the Lord more than those who
    watch for the morning,
more than those who watch for the morning.
In faith, let us turn to our God, whose love is sure.

CALL TO CONFESSION

Because of such great mercy,
God is ready to forgive
all the ways we fail to live in faithfulness.
Relying on that mercy,
let us confess our sin before God and one another.

PRAYER OF CONFESSION

Trusting you does not always come easy
when each day we are faced with the ugliness
    of the world.
We do not believe that love conquers fear.
We are not convinced that power comes
    through weakness.
We cannot conceive how you could heal us.
Forgive our lack of faith, O God,
and renew our trust in you,
for we would be disciples of Jesus,
in whose name we pray. Amen.

DECLARATION OF FORGIVENESS

If the Lord kept count of all our sins,
   who could stand?   *Ps. 130:3–4*
But with God there is forgiveness;
Christ gives us peace.
Thanks be to God!

PRAYER OF THE DAY

Almighty God,
in Jesus Christ you show us the breadth of
   your power   *Mark 5:28–29, 41*
and the depth of your love.
You listen to our cries of pain and hear our laments.   *2 Sam. 1:17;*
You see the fear in our eyes and know the secrets   *Ps. 130:1–2*
   of our hearts.
You do not turn from our distress, but stretch
   out your hand
to heal, to comfort, and to save.
All thanks and praise be to you, O God;
your steadfast love endures forever. **Amen.**

PRAYER FOR ILLUMINATION

By the power of your Spirit,
speak your Word to us, O God.
Show us who you are
and who you are calling us to be,
for the sake of your Son and our Lord, Jesus Christ. **Amen.**

PRAYERS OF INTERCESSION

[A time of silence is kept after each intercession.]
Knowing that God hears our prayers,
and trusting in the Spirit who intercedes with sighs
   too deep for words,   *Rom. 8:26*
let us pray together, saying,
Merciful God, hear our prayer.

Death is all around us, Lord;
the world groans with the weight of it.   *2 Sam. 1:17–27*
Hear our prayers for your warring world. . . .
Merciful God, **hear our prayer.**

The rulers of the nations need your wisdom, Lord;
oppression and injustice prevail.
Hear our prayers for the leaders of the world. . . .
Merciful God, **hear our prayer.**

The church is divided, Lord;
we fight and splinter.
Hear our prayers for the peace and unity of the church. . . .
Merciful God, **hear our prayer.**

Your children suffer, Lord;
they are hungry and can find no rest.
Hear our prayers for those who are poor or have no homes. . . .
Merciful God, **hear our prayer.**

We are sick, Lord,
and some of us are dying.
Hear our prayers for healing and peace. . . .
Merciful God, **hear our prayer.**

Our hearts are troubled, Lord;
guide us until we find our rest in you.
Hear our secret prayers. . . .
Merciful God, **hear our prayer.**

We give you thanks, O God,
for you are faithful and your love never ends.
Gather our prayers and conform them to your will,
we pray in Jesus' name. **Amen.**

INVITATION TO THE OFFERING

You know the generous act of our Lord Jesus Christ,   *2 Cor. 8:9*
that though he was rich,
yet for our sakes he became poor,
so that by his poverty we might become rich.
Sisters and brothers, let us give generously
of our goods and our lives
in imitation of our Lord and Savior.

PRAYER OF THANKSGIVING/DEDICATION
> Most holy God,
> who hears our prayers and answers them
> and gives us more than we can ask or imagine,
> accept these offerings and use them to your glory,
> that even now we might imitate your coming reign
> of justice, peace, and love,
> for the sake of Jesus Christ, our Lord. **Amen.**

CHARGE
> Go in peace,
> trusting even where you have not seen.

BLESSING
> May God our Guardian protect you,
> Christ the Healer restore you,
> and the Holy Spirit sustain you
> this day and forevermore.

Question for Reflection

In this week's readings, various people bring their suffering to God, through lament and the search for healing. How does Christ enable you—and how might you enable others—to be honest with God in doubt and pain?

Household Prayer: Morning

By your grace I arise from my bed this morning, Lord;
by the power of your Spirit I draw my breath.
As the dawn brightens into day,
enlighten my mind with your truth
and open my heart to all those I meet,
that I might reflect the light of Jesus Christ,
in whose name I give thanks and praise. Amen.

Household Prayer: Evening

As the night deepens, Lord, I give myself to your care.
For the ways you enabled me to live faithfully today, thank you.
For the ways I failed to follow Christ, forgive me.
And if I do not awaken in the morning,
receive me into your everlasting arms. Amen.

Proper 8

(Sunday between June 26 and July 2 inclusive)

COMPLEMENTARY

Wisdom of Solomon 1:13–15; 2:23–24   2 Corinthians
or Lamentations 3:22–33   8:7–15
Psalm 30   Mark 5:21–43

OPENING WORDS / CALL TO WORSHIP

Sing praises to God,   *Ps. 30:4, 7, 11*
give thanks for God's name.
For God clothes us with strength and joy
and God turns our mourning to dancing.
[or]
The steadfast love of the Lord never ceases;   *Lam. 3:22, 23*
God's mercies are everlasting.
They are new every morning.
Great is God's faithfulness.

CALL TO CONFESSION

Let us confess our sins to God,
for God is faithful and loves us eternally.

PRAYER OF CONFESSION

Holy God, we confess that we have sinned against you
and have strayed from living wholeheartedly.
Envy and fear have dulled our generosity,
and we have grown mean and destructive.
Forgive us our sins and return us to health
through the grace and mercy of Christ. Amen.

DECLARATION OF FORGIVENESS

Sisters and brothers, God loves us, forgives us,
and frees us from our sins;
therefore be at peace
and love with boldness and generosity.

PRAYER OF THANKSGIVING/DEDICATION

Holy God, thank you for giving us a joy for generosity
and a genuine love for those who are in need.
Pour out your Spirit upon these gifts and upon our lives
that together we may bring healing and hope to the world.
In Christ's name we pray. Amen.

CHARGE

My sisters and brothers, the Holy One has created you for good.
Delight in God, work for justice, and walk in peace.

BLESSING

May the blessing of God, who creates, redeems, and restores,
be with you now and always.

Questions for Reflection

When the woman who suffered a chronic and isolating ailment touched
Jesus, he stated that the power had gone out from him. What aspects of
your life and ministry empty you of power? How do you discern healthy
limits and habits for the care of yourself and others? Which spiritual
practices do you find most revitalizing when your energy reserves are
depleted? In such times, how does your faith make you whole?

Household Prayer: Morning

Good morning, God.
Before this day takes hold of me and I am spread too thin by care,
I come to you to sit quietly,
for you are good to those who wait for you,
to the soul that seeks your peace.
Fill me with your life-giving presence;
may all that I do this day be done with calm attention,
for you are my strength and peace. Amen.

PRAYER OF THE DAY

Steadfast God, you sent Jesus as witness
that no one is outside your healing reach.
Help us to trust in the abundance of your love
as we share your compassion and generosity
wherever we may go,
with you, in Christ, and through the Holy Spirit. **Amen.**

PRAYER FOR ILLUMINATION

Loving God, your Word has the power to restore our lives.
Open our hearts to the presence of your Spirit,
for you are mighty to save. **Amen.**

PRAYERS OF INTERCESSION

[Each petition may be followed with the words:
    *O Lover of souls, **restore our lives**.]*
Almighty God, you created the world for good;
give to all leaders and people
the wisdom to live in harmony with one another
for the health of all creation.
You call your church to abound in generosity;
inspire us to share our abundance
with our sister churches who are in need,
that together we may be a sign of unity in Christ.

Your touch has the power to make us whole;
restore all who suffer in body, mind, or spirit,
and strengthen us as we extend our arms in love
as witnesses to your healing.

Steadfast God, you call us to dwell with you forever.
We remember those who are dying and those who have died;
may they know the joy of your eternal presence,
Father, Son, and Holy Spirit. **Amen.**

INVITATION TO THE OFFERING

Let us joyfully share our abundance with others,
as we trust in God who provides for all our needs.

Complementary

Household Prayer: Evening

Thank you for helping me to become
a more generous and attentive person this day.
As I let go of all the things done and left undone this day,
make me mindful that it is your strength and steadfast loving presence
that keeps my faith whole and fills me with a quiet confidence. Amen.

Proper 9

(Sunday between July 3 and July 9 inclusive)

SEMICONTINUOUS

2 Samuel 5:1–5, 9–10   2 Corinthians 12:2–10
Psalm 48   Mark 6:1–13

OPENING WORDS / CALL TO WORSHIP

Jesus Christ, the crucified Lord,   *Mark. 1:14;*
calls us to believe the good news of salvation.   *2 Cor. 12:9*
His grace is sufficient for us.
Let us enter into God's new realm rejoicing,
not in our own strength,
but in the power of the Holy Spirit.
Let us worship God.

CALL TO CONFESSION

Threats to life pierce us
and cause us to doubt God's love.
But God shows his love for us   *Rom. 5:8*
in that while we were yet sinners
Christ died for us.
Let us confess our sins and receive new life.

PRAYER OF CONFESSION

Holy Three, Holy One, triune God,
we confess that we do not believe
that you have overcome sin and death.
We are more in touch with the pangs of our weakness
than we are with the power of your love.
In fear, we worship idols;
in despair, we collapse in hopelessness;
in rage, we seek to dominate others.
O God of David, forgive us.
O Son of David, have mercy on us.

**O Spirit of the Living God, grant us peace.
Send us out with the good news:
nothing can withstand the victory
of the cross and resurrection of Jesus Christ,
in whose name we pray. Amen.**

DECLARATION OF FORGIVENESS

Hear and believe this good news:
Jesus, the Christ, son of Mary,   *Mark 6:3; 14:22–24*
Son of the Most High God,
was broken and poured out
for our salvation.
In Jesus Christ our sins are forgiven. Amen.

PRAYER OF THE DAY

God the creator, God of the cross,
you show your power
in whirling galaxies and unseen forces.
You show your love
in the life, death, and resurrection of Jesus Christ.
Drive out the evils that threaten to break our spirits
and help us to rely on your all-sufficient grace,
for we pray in the name of Jesus Christ. **Amen.**

PRAYER FOR ILLUMINATION

Savior God,
you gave Zion as stronghold for David.
By the power of the Holy Spirit,
speak to us through Jesus Christ, your living Word,
in whose name we pray. **Amen.**

PRAYERS OF INTERCESSION

God of heaven and earth,
creator of all things seen and unseen,
we join with the church through all ages,
praying that you cast out all evil
and renew the face of the whole creation.

Grant wisdom and courage to the political leaders
so that they enact in every nation,

for the common good,
the justice you command.
Grant intelligence and generosity to leaders of business and industry
so that they provide dignity and safety
for every person and household on the planet.
Grant imagination and passion to educators and artists
so that they give clear guidance and true vision
enabling us to praise you
for the wonder and beauty of your world.
Grant compassion and skill to healers and caregivers
so that the sick and suffering may know your touch
as a foreshadowing of the resurrection.

We pray this day for all who are suffering
at the hands of the violent and power hungry,
the greedy and malicious,
the ignorant and misguided,
and the powers of evil beyond human control.
May each one who is afflicted
find comfort in your faith, hope, and love
to enable them to overcome these demonic attacks.

Empower your church with the Holy Spirit
to proclaim the gospel with authority,
for not even the gates of hell
can withstand the grace of Jesus Christ.

Complete the renewal you began
in raising Jesus from the dead.
Then will all creation shout with us,
Hallelujah! Amen.

INVITATION TO THE OFFERING
The Lord said to the apostle Paul,
My grace is sufficient for you. . . .   *2 Cor. 12:9a*
Jesus also said to Peter,
Every one to whom much is given,   *Luke 12:48b*
of him much will be required.
Let us bear witness to the love of God
by presenting our offerings of thanksgiving.

PRAYER OF THANKSGIVING/DEDICATION

Gracious triune God,
we thank you for the suffering love of Jesus Christ,
and for your presence with us
in times of joy and of sorrow,
sickness and health,
faithfulness and brokenness.
We bring these offerings as signs of our gratitude
and as tools in the ministry of the church.
Use them and us to make known the good news
of your healing love and renewing power,
in the name of Jesus Christ. **Amen.**

CHARGE

Show the love of God in all you do.
Be faithful witnesses to the grace of Jesus Christ.
Live in the power and joy of the Holy Spirit.

BLESSING

The Son of David lead you to his eternal kingdom;
the Son of Mary wipe all tears from your eyes;
the Son of the Most High God save you from all evil
and make you whole, now and forever.

Question for Reflection

Jesus charges his disciples to be vulnerable as he sends them out. The apostle Paul says that he embraces his vulnerability, "for whenever I am weak, then I am strong" (2 Cor. 12:10c). In what ways might God be calling you to be vulnerable today?

Household Prayer: Morning

Fire of life,
thank you for bringing me safely through the night.
As this new day dawns
let me receive it as a gift and a blessing.
Open my mind and senses to be fully awake to you.
Attune my body to the rhythms of the day
so that I can love and serve others as you guide me.

If I experience hardship or pain
or if I am exposed to danger,
send your Holy Spirit to help me
to put my trust more fully in you.
Remind me that in life and in death
I belong to you.
Let me walk gently on the earth,
thankful for your providence and grace.
Let me dance joyfully with you,
mindful that I share movement with planets and stars.
When the day is done and it is time to rest,
grant that I can offer the day to you with thanksgiving.
I offer my prayer in the name of the Beloved Son,
Jesus Christ the Lord. Amen.

Household Prayer: Evening

Holy One,
I lift my evening prayer
as shadows cover me
and night sounds come from hidden places.
But darkness is not dark to you,
so I ask that you hear my prayers
and see me through the night.
I have only the activities of the day
to offer as my living sacrifice of praise.
Forgive my unholiness;
reconcile me by your grace.
For the sake of the risen Christ,
this night grant me peace. Amen.

Proper 9

(Sunday between July 3 and July 9 inclusive)

COMPLEMENTARY

Ezekiel 2:1–5	2 Corinthians 12:2–10
Psalm 123	Mark 6:1–13

OPENING WORDS / CALL TO WORSHIP
God is mighty in word and deed.
God's mercy is everlasting.
Blessed be the one holy and living God.
Glory to God forever.

CALL TO CONFESSION
Let us confess our sins to God,   *2 Cor. 12:9*
whose power is made perfect in our weakness.

PRAYER OF CONFESSION
Holy God, you call us to boldly proclaim your name,   *Ezek. 2:3–4*
yet we are stubborn and rebellious and heedless
**   of your call.**
By the power of your Spirit, raise us to new life
that we may return to faithful living,
in Christ's name we pray. Amen.

DECLARATION OF FORGIVENESS
Sisters and brothers, God's grace and mercy are
    never ending.
Your sins are forgiven, therefore be at peace.

PRAYER OF THE DAY
O God of grace and mercy,
you call us to proclaim your healing
and faithfully fulfill your kingdom mission.

Let us not count the cost of our wins and losses,
but keep our eyes fixed on you
as we seek your realm of peace. **Amen.**

PRAYER FOR ILLUMINATION

Come, Holy Spirit;
when we become stubborn and unbelieving,
open hearts to receive your Word,
then set us free to follow in the power of Christ's love. **Amen.**

PRAYERS OF INTERCESSION

[Each petition may be followed by the words:
  Loving God, have mercy on us.]
Almighty God, who transforms our weakness
    into strength,
receive the prayers we lovingly offer on behalf of
    the church and the world.

Our world is an anxious place divided by ideologies,   *Ezek. 2:4*
and we grow more stubborn and impertinent
    each day.
Break down the barriers that exist among
    peoples and nations;
restore and strengthen our common life.

Give to your church a bold vision and a daring love   *Mark 6:8–9*
to speak and act on behalf of your mission
to restore all people and creation in peace.
Teach us to trust simplicity and travel light together.

Comfort all who suffer in body, mind, or spirit.
Expand our compassion, increase our faith,
    and make us whole
as we work together for the healing of those in need.

Eternal God, we remember those who are dying
and those who have died.
Draw them in to your heavenly realm with you,
Christ, and the Holy Spirit,
that they may dwell with you in paradise. **Amen.**

INVITATION TO THE OFFERING

Jesus calls us to travel light as we serve the world, *Mark 6:7–9*
for God is our strength and provision.
Let us faithfully bring our offerings to God.

PRAYER OF THANKSGIVING/DEDICATION

Divine Giver, all that we have is a gift from you,
and your grace is our sufficiency.
Pour out your Spirit upon these gifts
that they may increase your blessing to others,
through the grace and mercy of Christ. **Amen.**

CHARGE

Fear not, for God's power is perfected in our weakness. *2 Cor. 12:10*
Go in God's strength to love and serve.

BLESSING

May the love of God,
the power of Christ,
and the fellowship of the Holy Spirit
dwell richly in you forever.

Questions for Reflection

Stuff distracts us. Useless clutter we think we cannot live without can be
a burden: too many coats, shoes, garden tools, or mismatched kitchen
storage containers with no lids in sight as they tumble out of overstuffed
cabinets. Perhaps our clutter shows up in other ways: on a computer that
has grown slow from processing too many useless files, or when our minds
grow dull from too much Web surfing or television viewing. Do you
struggle with too much stuff? How do Jesus' words about traveling light
challenge you to change the way you live? How can you follow him more
faithfully today?

Household Prayer: Morning

Loving God, as this day opens into new and untold possibility,
purge me of my compulsive need to carry useless baggage—
physically, mentally, or emotionally.
Teach me to walk simply with you
as I trust in your abundant provision. Amen.

Household Prayer: Evening

Lord, as I come to the close of this day,
I thank you for the gift of attentiveness
and for every moment that the eye of my heart was fixed on you.
When I failed, you were with me,
and when I wavered, you were there,
for there is no place that you are not.
And so I rest in peace this night,
for your grace is more than sufficient for me. Amen.

Proper 10

(Sunday between July 10 and July 16 inclusive)

SEMICONTINUOUS

2 Samuel 6:1–5, 12b–19   Ephesians 1:3–14
Psalm 24   Mark 6:14–29

OPENING WORDS / CALL TO WORSHIP
Come, let us worship God   *2 Sam. 6:5, 14;*
with the passion and joy of King David   *Eph. 1:3b*
   and all the people
who sang and danced before the ark of the covenant.
Let us worship our Savior
with the songs of praise and thanksgiving of
   the apostle Paul
and all who are blessed with every spiritual blessing.
God has blessed us in our Lord Jesus Christ,
destined us to be children of God,
and sealed us in the Holy Spirit.
Let us worship God.

CALL TO CONFESSION
The godliness of Jesus Christ   *Eph. 1:4, 7*
calls us to be holy and blameless.
The riches of God's grace
promise forgiveness of our trespasses.
Let us confess our sins.

PRAYER OF CONFESSION
Holy, holy, holy Lord,
you are the God of glory.
We confess that we often forget
that your holiness is dangerous.
We take our impurities for granted,
make excuses for the sins we commit,

71

and expect you to overlook the harm we cause
while still demanding justice from others.
We do not deserve your mercy.
Forgive us,
and return us to a right relationship with you
for the sake of your Son, Jesus Christ.
You made us for the purpose of praising you;
enliven us with the Holy Spirit
so that we can fulfill our calling
in the name of our Lord Jesus Christ. Amen.

DECLARATION OF FORGIVENESS

According to the riches of his grace,   *Eph. 1:7, 13d*
which God has lavished upon us
and sealed for us by the promised Holy Spirit,
hear this good news:
In Jesus Christ, you are forgiven.

PRAYER OF THE DAY

Holy Trinity,
yours is the justice
that calls power to account.
Yours is the love
that calls sinners to repent.
Yours is the mercy
that forgives us and grants us eternal life.
Lead us in the truth about the Beloved,
and set us free to rejoice with all our might
over the great mystery you have revealed:
that you are bringing all things into harmony
through Jesus Christ the Lord. **Amen.**

PRAYER FOR ILLUMINATION

Spirit of the living God,
seal in us your Word of truth,
the gospel of salvation,
so that we can faithfully follow
and joyfully serve
our Lord Jesus Christ,
for it is in his name that we pray. **Amen.**

PRAYERS OF INTERCESSION

[Silence is kept between intercessions.]
Holy Abba of our Lord Jesus Christ,
who sends the Holy Spirit
to help us in our praying,
open our senses to your creation
and our hearts to the needs of others.

Grant us faith, hope, and imagination
to see your vision of the fullness of time
when weapons will be crushed by peace,
stomachs will be filled
by abundant harvests generously shared,
and thirsts quenched by pure rain
falling from clean skies;
diseases will be healed,
minds made clear,
and bodies made new,
so that all things reveal oneness in Christ.

Even now, Abba,
empower us by the Spirit to serve Christ in love
by sharing your vision
and working in the world
for which Christ died and rose and prays
and is coming to complete in resurrection.
We pray these things in the name of our Lord Jesus Christ. **Amen**.

INVITATION TO THE OFFERING

Consider what God has given to us in Jesus Christ;
remember that, even now, the Holy Spirit dwells in us;
rejoice that we are part of God's plan for all time.
Let us present our offerings of thanksgiving.

PRAYER OF THANKSGIVING/DEDICATION

Glorious God,
you created us because you are love.
It is your will and our destiny that we live
into the full humanity of Jesus Christ
so that we can praise you,

give voice to creation's joy,
and join with all things in heaven and on earth
to rejoice in your goodness forever.
Thank you for this high calling and privilege.
We bring an offering taken from the gifts you have given us.
Because they come from you, they are holy;
because you have given them to us,
you honor us as if we are holy.
As we return them to you with our thanksgiving,
bless them with the power of your love
so that they may touch the lives of others
and inspire them to join us
in giving you thanks and praise
in the name of Jesus Christ, the King of glory. **Amen.**

CHARGE

Do not hold back the power of the Spirit;
celebrate with all your might
Christ's victory over sin and death.
Be brave and tell the truth about evil.
Serve the weak;
comfort the grieving;
encourage the despairing;
honor everyone to whom respect is due.
Remember that in life and in death,
body and soul, you belong to God,
who promises resurrection
in Jesus Christ.

BLESSING

May the Holy Trinity fill you with joy,
surround you with peace,
and lead you to eternal life.

Question for Reflection

The lectionary readings suggest comparing the exuberant dancing and merrymaking of David to Paul's enthusiastic description of the Christian's calling, while contrasting these to the deathly revelries of Herod's court. How do you know which present-day occasions to celebrate with all your might and which to speak out against?

Household Prayer: Morning

Creator of light,
I greet you as the morning dawns.
Thank you for this new day.
May it be for me a sign
and an anticipation of your coming kingdom.
Fill me with the energy I will need
to love all whom I meet today.
I pray that I harm no one
and that I may have the mind of Christ
as I live in the world he came to save.
Receive my body, mind, and spirit
as a living sacrifice of thanksgiving
for the love you show me in Jesus Christ.
And where my wholeness is broken
by sin or sickness or the weight of the day,
let me seek you in repentance,
reach out to you for healing,
and lay my burdens before your throne of grace.
When the time for rest comes,
let me find my repose in you,
my comfort in life
and my hope of life everlasting,
through Jesus Christ my Lord. Amen.

Household Prayer: Evening

Faithful God,
where I am now
the earth is turning away from the sun
so that for other parts of the world,
the day is just beginning.
Thank you for abiding with us
through the day and through the night.
As I gather up thoughts of the hours just past
and reflect on what, if anything, they mean,
guide my meditations.
There were times when you used me
to love someone with Christ's love,

to encourage someone with a word from the Spirit,
to comfort someone with your tender touch,
to challenge someone with your mighty arm.
Let me not be proud, arrogant, or boastful.
Let me rejoice in your goodness and mercy.
I have sinned against you and others this day.
I am sorry.
By your Spirit, help me to turn away from my sins.
Forgive me through the grace of Jesus Christ.
Let me go to my rest this night in peace,
trusting not in my own goodness,
but rejoicing in your glory.
If it is your will,
let me rise to a new day,
giving thanks and praise to you,
the triune God, now and forever. Amen.

Proper 10

(Sunday between July 10 and July 16 inclusive)

COMPLEMENTARY

Amos 7:7–15	Ephesians 1:3–14
Psalm 85:8–13	Mark 6:14–29

OPENING WORDS / CALL TO WORSHIP

God has accomplished all things through Christ,   *Eph. 1:5, 11–12*
so that we might live as God's own children.
Let us give thanks to God
and live for the praise of God's glory.

CALL TO CONFESSION

Jesus loves us with steadfast tenderness;
therefore, let us confess our sins to God.

PRAYER OF CONFESSION

Holy God,
you call us to be your beloved children and to
    care for one another,
yet we fail to love others and ourselves.
Helpless and ashamed, we turn our hearts to you.
Forgive us, and then tenderly teach us
to stand strong and courageous in the fullness
    of your love,
by the grace and mercy of Christ. Amen.

DECLARATION OF FORGIVENESS

Sisters and brothers, God forgives us and
    strengthens us for love;
therefore be at peace.

PRAYER OF THE DAY

Eternal God, from the foundation of the world,   *Amos 7:7–8*
you have set a plumb line to measure our lives
so that we may live in truth.
By the power of your Holy Spirit,
strengthen our hands for building justice and
     making peace
through the righteousness of Christ. **Amen.**

PRAYER FOR ILLUMINATION

Loving God, your Word brings peace to all who
     turn to you.
Send your Holy Spirit to dwell among us
that we might praise Christ's glory. **Amen.**

PRAYERS OF INTERCESSION

Almighty God, you have set a plumb line   *Amos 7:7;*
from the foundation of the world to lead us   *Eph. 1:4*
     into truth.
Receive our prayers of hope and healing
on behalf of the church and the world.

Give wisdom to all leaders and people
to resist the earthly powers of fear and violence
that destroy our common life.
In the face of injustice, oppression, and brutal power,
strengthen our wavering wills to stand in the power of Christ.

Stir up in us the power to care for your creation,
not as resources to be exploited,
but as a precious gift to be held in trust
as a revelation of your faithfulness.

Inspire your church to share Christ's love
beyond the safety of its walls,
and fill us with an infectious joy for sharing your gospel
as we welcome your coming reign.

Bring healing and wholeness to all
who are haunted by broken relationships, abuse,
illness, or terror and trauma of any kind;
restore us in your peace.

Eternal God, in Christ you gather all things up
in heaven and on earth;
enfold all those who will be born this day
and all those who will die into the joy
of your never-ending realm of peace,
for our hope is set on Christ as we live to praise his glory. **Amen.**

INVITATION TO THE OFFERING
The Lord gives what is good
and makes a pathway for generosity to follow.
Let us walk in the righteousness of Christ
as we bring our gifts to God.

PRAYER OF THANKSGIVING/DEDICATION
Thank you for filling us with every spiritual grace
that we might be a blessing for others.
Consecrate the gifts we offer for the increase of your love.
May they bring blessing to others
and praise to your glorious name. Amen.

CHARGE
Go forth in joy and peace, for you are God's beloved.

BLESSING
May the God of our Lord Jesus Christ,
who has blessed us in Christ,
fill you with every blessing through the power of the Holy Spirit.

Questions for Reflection

To experience one's self as God's beloved is a gift beyond compare. For
some, it is difficult to receive such a gift; for others, such grace comes more
easily. How can we deepen our experience of that gift in ourselves? How
might we encourage this gift in others?

Household Prayer: Morning

O God of steadfast love and faithfulness,
as I awaken this day in expectation,
I turn my heart toward you, for I am your beloved.
Fill me with your wisdom and insight,
and guide my feet into the way of peace
as I walk your righteous path. Amen.

Household Prayer: Evening

Recounting both the blessings and challenges of this day,
I give thanks to you, O God,
for my hope is in Christ who makes all things new,
and so I rest this night. Amen.

Proper 11

(Sunday between July 17 and July 23 inclusive)

SEMICONTINUOUS

2 Samuel 7:1–14a	Ephesians 2:11–22
Psalm 89:20–37	Mark 6:30–34, 53–56

OPENING WORDS / CALL TO WORSHIP
Come into the presence of the Most High God
with songs of praise and shouts of thanksgiving.
For our Savior frees us from slavery;
our Savior heals our diseases;
our Savior is our peace.
You are a holy temple in the Lord Jesus Christ.   *Eph. 2:22*
Come; let us worship God.

CALL TO CONFESSION
Even our best intentions go awry
when we are not at one with God's purpose.
Our gracious God journeys with us
and provides for us
with unending mercy, patience, and kindness
so that when we repent,
we find ourselves forgiven.
Let us confess our sins.

PRAYER OF CONFESSION
Eternal God, your steadfast love endures forever.
We confess that we act as if we are in control
as if you will bless whatever we do.
If we think of others at all,
it is with an eye
toward their usefulness to us.
If we consider your creation,
it is to ponder what benefits us.

81

We have failed to show your love
or to do justice in obedience to you.
We have no right to be called your children.
Have mercy on us, God of grace.
Lord, have mercy.
Forgive our sins, we humbly pray.
Put the mind of Christ within us, O God,   *Phil. 2:5*
so that our lives take the form of a cross.
Use us to break down walls of hostility   *Eph. 2:14*
within the church,
among the nations,
and around the world.
Equip us to do your will,
giving you glory, honor, and praise
together with the Son and the Holy Spirit,
one God forever and ever. Amen.

DECLARATION OF FORGIVENESS
Our Lord Jesus gives us rest and peace.
Our Master's touch heals us,
and his shed blood is our salvation.
In Jesus Christ, our sins are forgiven. **Amen.**

PRAYER OF THE DAY
O Trinity,
fill our weakness with your strength;
bind up our brokenness with your unity;
calm our fears and our dread of dying
with your peace.
Let us be about the tasks of your love.
Use us to build a holy place
where healing and caring and joy
blend in the tones of worship
to the glory of your holy name. **Amen.**

PRAYER FOR ILLUMINATION
Holy Spirit,
come and dwell in us.
Place Jesus Christ in us
so that he is the cornerstone   *Eph. 2:20b*

holding us together
and making us a sacred place
where steadfast love and faithfulness will meet;   *Ps. 85:10*
righteousness and peace will kiss each other.
We pray in Jesus' name. **Amen**.

PRAYERS OF INTERCESSION

O God, merciful and just;
O God, kind and compassionate;
O God, forever faithful
for your own name's sake:
we pray for the world
Christ came to save;
we pray for the kingdom
you are bringing through Christ.
Bless the church, the body of Christ,
with the power of the Holy Spirit,
so that our strength is renewed like the eagle's.
Then send us out to proclaim the good news
that in Jesus Christ there is newness of life.

We pray for all who are weary from hard labor,
especially for those who are not fairly paid,
for those who work in dangerous places,
for those trapped in slavery.
Break yokes of oppression and bonds of bitterness.

We pray for all who serve on behalf of others,
especially for those who care for the sick,
    elderly, and dying;
for those who fight fires, enforce just laws,
    serve in the military;
for those who hold public office.
Build up all people in peace and freedom.

We pray for ourselves,
that we will be faithful,
especially in times of temptation;
that our diseases will be healed,
so we have strength to serve others;

that our love for one another and you
   grow ever deeper.
Make us into a holy temple in the Lord;   *Eph. 2:21, 22*
build us spiritually into a dwelling place for God—
into your kingdom, O Holy Trinity. **Amen.**

INVITATION TO THE OFFERING
Unless God builds the house,   *Ps. 127:1–2*
those who build labor in vain.
God gives rest to the weary
and sleep for his beloved.
Let us present offerings of thanksgiving,
without fear or anxiety about anything,
for God provides for us.

PRAYER OF THANKSGIVING/DEDICATION
Almighty God,
enthroned in eternity;
crucified and risen Christ,
dwelling in heaven and with your people;
powerful Holy Spirit,
bringing life and truth;
we thank you
for calling us when we had no hope
and for crowning us with salvation.
We thank you
for enriching our lives with all that is good
and for providing for us in times of trial.
Make us ever more mindful
of the blessings you grant us each day;
deepen our trust in your love and mercy.
Increase our thanksgiving
by guiding our offerings to help others in need.
Unite us all in a community of thanksgiving,
always glorifying you,
O Holy Trinity, now and forever. **Amen.**

CHARGE

Seek out your neighbor in love.
If it is within your power,
be reconciled to your enemies.
Hunger and thirst for the rule of Christ Jesus
and let him dwell in your minds and hearts.

BLESSING

God grant you peace in your sleeping and waking;
Christ fill you with joy in your working and playing;
the Holy Spirit drive you with passion in your love for God.

Question for Reflection

God promised to build King David into a "house." Paul told the Ephesians that in Christ they would be built into "a dwelling place for God." How is the Holy Spirit living in you?

Household Prayer: Morning

Holy One who is Holy Three,
I praise you as I rise from my bed.
As the morning dew glistens
and songbirds greet the day,
let my prayers go up to you.
Awaken my body to the wonder of life
and fill my spirit with the joy of your presence.
I seek your guidance as I prepare for activity;
instruct me on what is necessary
and what is fruitless
so that I wisely use the gifts you give me.
Let me see all people as your beloved children,
some needing care,
some needing forgiveness,
all deserving dignity, respect, and hospitality.
If it is your will,
protect me from harm.
In all events,
grant me the comfort of your presence
so that I can faithfully obey your will.

Spare others suffering because of my sinfulness.
Let me bear witness to your goodness
in my words, my actions, and my silences
so that you can use me
to draw others into your presence.
Bring us together into the time
when Christ Jesus comes
and all sorrows are wiped away.
Then all will be one
and joined to you in love
by the grace of our same Lord Jesus Christ,
who, together with you and the Holy Spirit,
is worshiped and glorified now and forever. Amen.

Household Prayer: Evening

Majesty of holiness,
thank you for another day
lived in your grace.
Thank you for all whom I met
who showed me your kindness.
Help me to repent of my sins
before I go to my bed this night.
Let me receive the blessing of forgiveness
and enter a period of rest
with the burdens of the day
lifted from me,
and the comfort of your peace
as a pillow for my head.
If it is your will,
speak to me as I sleep,
and let me remember your words
as I rise to a new day,
giving you thanks and praise,
one God in three persons forever. Amen.

Proper 11

(Sunday between July 17 and July 23 inclusive)

COMPLEMENTARY

Jeremiah 23:1–6   Ephesians 2:11–22
Psalm 23   Mark 6:30–34, 53–56

OPENING WORDS / CALL TO WORSHIP
Christ says, come away to a deserted place
    and rest a while.   *Mark 6:31*
God calls us to quiet and rest,
even as we continue to minister to those in need.

CALL TO CONFESSION
Let us confess our sin, confident in God's love for us.

PRAYER OF CONFESSION
God of green pastures,   *Ps. 23:2, 3*
we confess that we can get so busy and distracted
that we lose sight of your love and care for us.
We forget to live in gratitude
and fail to live lives of goodness and mercy.
Forgive us, heal us, and lead us down gentle paths
that restore our souls. Amen.

DECLARATION OF FORGIVENESS
As your brother/sister in Christ,   *Ps. 23:3*
I remind you that you have been restored
to the grace of God.
Therefore let us share a sign of peace with
    one another,
for this congregation is the feast that God has
    prepared for us.

PRAYER OF THE DAY

Holy One, we want to be the sheep of your pasture.   *Jer. 23:1*
Care for us, feed us, and lead us, we pray.
Once we are strengthened by your presence,
raise us up to be shepherds ourselves   *Jer. 23:4*
who tend to those who fear and dismay
so that our lives may reflect our Good Shepherd,
    Jesus Christ. **Amen.**

PRAYER FOR ILLUMINATION

May the reading of your Word
draw near to you those of us once far off.   *Eph. 2:13*
May the hearing of your Word
break down the dividing walls between us,
for Jesus Christ, your living Word, is our peace. **Amen.**   *Eph. 2:14*

PRAYERS OF INTERCESSION

God of Jesus Christ and our God,
we are no longer strangers and aliens,   *Eph. 2:19–20*
but citizens with the saints of the commonwealth
    of God,
built on the foundation of the apostles and prophets.
In Christ we are joined together as a dwelling place
    for God.   *Eph. 2:21*

We pray for those who have been called or
    elected as leaders,
that they may be guided by your voice and by the voices
    of their people.
In Christ we are joined together as a dwelling place
    for God.

We pray for the pastors and teachers of the church,
that they may faithfully tend and not scatter those
    entrusted to them.   *Jer. 23:2*
In Christ we are joined together as a dwelling place
    for God.

We pray for those who are poor and in need
    of assistance,
and for ourselves that we may tenderly care for them.

In Christ we are joined together as a dwelling place for God.

We pray for the victims of war and other forms
  of violence,
that we may be good news for them both in word
  and in deed.
**In Christ we are joined together as a dwelling place
  for God.**

We pray for the sick and infirm and those who are
  spiritually hungry,
that we may be a message of compassion.   *Mark 6:34*
**In Christ we are joined together as a dwelling place
  for God.**

Today we pray especially for children and others
who have been abused by clergy,   *Jer. 23:1*
that we may be quick to care for them
and build systems of accountability.
**In Christ we are joined together as a dwelling place
  for God.**

Good Shepherd, Lord of Righteousness,
bring us together through the cross of Christ   *Eph. 2:16*
and break down the dividing walls between us.
Be our peace,   *Eph. 2:14*
and by your Holy Spirit
renew our citizenship in your kingdom. **Amen.**

INVITATION TO THE OFFERING
God spreads a table of blessings before us.   *Ps. 23:5*
Let us express our gratitude
by giving a portion of what has been given to us.

PRAYER OF THANKSGIVING/DEDICATION
God of green pastures and still waters,   *Ps. 23:2*
bless these gifts that we have been given
that they may become part of your banquet
  for the world. **Amen.**

CHARGE

Let the Spirit build us together into a living temple
for the Lord!   *Eph. 2:21*

BLESSING

We have been restored in the worship of our God.
Have no fear, for God is with us.
We are dwelling in the house of the Lord—
let us be God's banquet for one another!

Questions for Reflection

The Old Testament year of jubilee that Jesus refers to in his first sermon—
what some have called his "mission statement"—was a time set aside every
forty-nine years to forgive financial debt and redistribute the land among
the people. Why do you think God envisioned a year of jubilee? What
might that look like in our world today?

Household Prayer: Morning

Holy One, thank you for the gift of this new day.
Please help me to stay mindful of your creation
and your teachings as I travel through it.
Empower me to see and spread
the good news of your grace for all people. Amen.

Household Prayer: Evening

Holy One, thank you for the gift of today.
Thank you for all the ways
that I saw your glory and learned your teachings
beyond speech and words.
As I drift to sleep this night,
may the meditations of my heart
draw me closer to you,
my Rock and my Redeemer. Amen.

Proper 12

(Sunday between July 24 and July 30 inclusive)

SEMICONTINUOUS

2 Samuel 11:1–15	Ephesians 3:14–21
Psalm 14	John 6:1–21

OPENING WORDS / CALL TO WORSHIP
God created
all things visible and invisible; none other.
God provides
food for your stomach and spirit; none other.
God is able to accomplish abundantly   *Eph. 3:19*
far more than all we can ask or imagine.
Let us worship the Trinity, and none other.

CALL TO CONFESSION
Atheists are not the only foolish people   *Ps. 14:1*
who act as if there is no God.
Even in the midst of the miracles of life,
we often do not acknowledge God's presence.
And yet the Spirit is with us as the source of life.
Therefore, let us confess our sins and receive Christ's mercy.

PRAYER OF CONFESSION
God of wonder,
Lord of King David
and of the Son, the Messiah, David's greater son,
we confess our sins and pray for your help
so that we can truly repent and turn from evil.
Deliver us from the temptation
to hide from you, to lie to you, or to excuse ourselves
because of the harm we have done to others.
Forgive us for the curse
we have brought upon the earth.

Restore your creation to full health
and feed the multitudes from the abundance
of your merciful power.
Grow in us a deeper desire
to love Christ with the fullness of your love,
and to glorify him, along with you and the Holy Spirit,
now and forever. Amen.

DECLARATION OF FORGIVENESS

The river of God's mercy
runs deeper and wider than our sin.
God removes our sins
as far as the heavens   *Ps. 103:11–12*
are above the earth.
Beloved in the risen Christ,
we are forgiven. **Amen.**

PRAYER OF THE DAY

Triune God,
shepherd of your people Israel,
you provide for us far more
than we expect or imagine possible.
Calm our fears;
speak peace to us;
lead us beyond ourselves.
Gather us with all the saints in the church
to glorify you for your mighty deeds.
We pray in the strong name of Jesus Christ. **Amen.**

PRAYER FOR ILLUMINATION

O Holy Spirit, creative power of God,
strengthen us to the depths of our humanity.
Help us to overcome temptations to abuse our neighbors;
fill us with the love of Christ.
Feed us the bread of heaven
so that we will share with the world
the saying that is true,
I AM is with us.
We pray in the name of Jesus Christ,
Son of God, Savior. **Amen.**

PRAYERS OF INTERCESSION

O Lord, have mercy upon us;
O Christ, have mercy upon us;
O Spirit, have mercy upon us,
and grant us your peace.
We pray for those who have no peace:
for children, women, and men
whose homes have been destroyed by war;
whose minds have been damaged
by what they have seen or felt or done;
who are hungry or thirsty or ill
because they are refugees or poor
or underpaid or trapped in human trafficking.
We pray for those whom you have called to be peacemakers:
leaders of governments and businesses
and nongovernmental organizations;
leaders of the church and scholars
and scientists and educators;
community organizers and citizens
and everyone of sound mind and body
who can bear the burdens of the weak.
Give us strength and courage and faith
to trust Jesus Christ and to be Christlike
for the good of the creation you are redeeming
and to the glory of the One who redeems all,
who, with you and the Holy Spirit, we worship
now and forever. **Amen.**

INVITATION TO THE OFFERING

As God provides seed for the sower   *Isa. 55:10d*
and bread for the eater,
so has God provided enough
for us to share
as we give thanks and praise
through our Lord, Jesus Christ.
Let us present tithes and offerings.

PRAYER OF THANKSGIVING/DEDICATION

O God, creator of rain and sun and soil,
ruler of nations,
thank you for the abundance of the earth.
We know there is enough food
to feed everyone alive today;
we are grateful that there are cures
for the most common diseases;
we praise you for the witness of Jesus Christ,
who showed no lust for power or riches.
Fill the world with the Spirit of Christ
so that food, medicine, and peace flow as freely
as the river of life from the throne of the Lamb.   *Rev. 22:1-2*
Bless our offerings
so that we can follow where Christ leads,
freeing the wealth of nations   *Isa. 60*
for the service of the kingdom.
We pray in Jesus' name. **Amen**.

CHARGE

Share the bread of life with all whom you meet;
let the Spirit of life strengthen your whole being;
and be open to the transforming of your soul
by the fullness of God.

BLESSING

God feed you with open hands,
protect you with mighty arms,
heal you with gentle fingers.
The scent of bread, fish, and grace
linger in the clothing of your heart
and renew your faith
when strong sea winds blow.

Question for Reflection

How does Christ feed you today?

Household Prayer: Morning

Praise to you, O God most holy, Uncreated Light.
I am thankful that in you there is no night.
Let my morning prayer rise to you
as blooming flowers turn to meet the sun.
May I meet the adventure of this day
open to the opportunities you give me
to show the love and justice of Jesus Christ.
May I be so filled with the Holy Spirit
that peace and compassion radiate from me
to bless others so that they are touched by your glory.
Enrich my senses with the beauty of your world,
my mind with wonder at your ways,
and my spirit with gratitude for all
that you prepare for the redemption of creation
through Jesus Christ the Son.
Pierce my heart with love,
especially for those in any kind of need,
so that I am moved to help where I can
and moved to cry out for help
if the need is greater than I can answer.
Spare others the consequences of my sin,
and help me to be reconciled
with those I have harmed in the past.
Make me slow to anger, quick to forgive,
and quicker still to confess my faults.
In all things, let me trust in you.
Let me finish the day as I begin it,
in your care—
in your gentle, merciful, loving hands,
beloved and blessed triune God,
whom I would worship and adore
now and forever. Amen.

Household Prayer: Evening

Holy triune God,
Lord, have mercy,
Lord, have mercy,
Lord, have mercy.
Thank you for the love
you have shown me today.
The gifts of air, water, food, and clothing;
the gifts of human and nonhuman companionship and community;
the gift of the Spirit around me and Christ within me:
all these gifts call for my deepest, highest praise to you.
Forgive me
for the times today when I have failed
to follow your guidance,
submit to your rule,
or glory in your majesty.
Grant healing and peace
to any whom I have harmed today;
let them not suffer because of my sins.
Let us enter the night together,
giving praise for your mercy and kindness.
Grant that we will journey into night,
led by your eternal Light,
and that we may gain comfort, rest, and renewal,
rising to a new day giving you thanks and praise
until you bring resurrection to all creation. Amen.

Proper 12

(Sunday between July 24 and July 30 inclusive)

COMPLEMENTARY

2 Kings 4:42–44	Ephesians 3:14–21
Psalm 145:10–18	John 6:1–21

OPENING WORDS / CALL TO WORSHIP
Your creation gives thanks to you, O God.   *Ps. 145:10–12*
And we, your faithful, bless you.
We shall speak of the glory of your realm and
    tell of your power.
**We shall let all people know your mighty deeds
    and glorious splendor.**

CALL TO CONFESSION
Let us confess to our God,   *Ps. 145:17–18*
for the Lord is just in all his ways
and kind in all his doings.
The Lord is near to all who call on him,
to all who call on him in truth.

PRAYER OF CONFESSION
God, you uphold those who are falling   *Ps. 145:14*
and raise up all who are bowed down.
Therefore we confess our sins—
both things we have done and
things we have left undone—
in every confidence that
you will open your hands to us   *Ps. 145:16*
in an embrace of forgiveness and love. Amen.

DECLARATION OF FORGIVENESS
Dearly beloved,   *Eph. 3:16–19*
through the power of the Spirit that is at work within us

God forgives our sins and strengthens our inner beings.
So now live knowing the love of Christ,
which surpasses all knowledge
and fills us with the fullness of God.

PRAYER OF THE DAY

Generous God, you give us what we need   *Ps. 145:15–16*
and satisfy our desires in due season.
Grant that our inner beings may be strengthened   *Eph. 3:16–17*
through your Spirit,
and that Christ may dwell in our hearts
through faith,
that you may accomplish within us
far more than all we ask or can imagine. **Amen.**   *Eph. 3:19–20*

PRAYER FOR ILLUMINATION

Holy God, may this your Word
give us the power to comprehend,   *Eph. 3:18–19*
with all the saints,
the length and width, the height and depth
    of the love of Christ and fullness of life in you. **Amen.**

PRAYERS OF INTERCESSION

God of abundance,
you open your hand and feed us in due season,   *Ps. 145:15–16*
satisfying the desires of every living thing.
**You are just in all your ways, and kind in
    all your doings.**   *Ps. 145:17*

We pray for the family of nations,
the families in our communities, and our
    own families,   *Eph. 3:15*
that they may have all they need to live in peace
    and harmony.
**You are just in all your ways, and kind in
    all your doings.**

We pray for all churches and denominations,
that we may find ways of cooperating
to care for the earth,
and care for those in need,
while giving you the glory in all that we do. *Eph. 3:21*
You are just in all your ways, and kind in
all your doings.

God, you are near to all who call out to you.
Use us, as you used the boy with two fish and
five barley loaves, *John 6:9*
to answer the cries of the hungry.
You are just in all your ways, and kind in
all your doings.

We pray for the victims of war and violence,
for the orphans, mothers, and men who must live
on the streets,
and for all those who are seen as the fragments
of society. *John 6:12*
May they be gathered up so that no one is lost.
You are just in all your ways, and kind in
all your doings.

We pray for the sick and those facing the end
of their days.
May Christ dwell in their hearts through faith,
and may they know that they are rooted and
grounded in love. *Eph. 3:17*
You are just in all your ways, and kind in
all your doings.

When we would make you a king, forgive us. *John 6:15*
When we are caught up in the storms of life,
come to us, calm our fears, and help us to reach
our destinations. *John 6:20–21*
Now through the power of the Holy Spirit,
and in the love of Christ,
to you be the glory in the church for all generations. **Amen.** *Eph. 3:21*

INVITATION TO THE OFFERING

Because a little boy shared his bread and fish,
a multitude ate.   *John 6:11*
Let us share what has been given to us.

PRAYER OF THANKSGIVING/DEDICATION

We rejoice with thanksgiving for all we have received.
Multiply these gifts that we give
so that the world may more deeply know
fullness of life in you. **Amen.**

CHARGE

Go now, rooted and grounded in love,   *Eph. 3:17*
to make known to all people
the mighty deeds of God!   *Ps. 145:12*

BLESSING

We have been upheld and raised up by our God.   *Ps. 145:14*
May God continue to strengthen your inner being   *Eph. 3:16*
and carry you out into the splendor of God's kingdom.

Question for Reflection

There is much hunger in the world, and many people live in want. Even the earth is wounded by humans and not getting what it needs to recover. In that context, how do you receive the word of the psalmist who writes, "The eyes of all look to you, and you give them their food in due season. You open your hand, satisfying the desire of every living thing" (Ps. 145:15–16)?

Household Prayer: Morning

God of the sunrise,
ground me and root me in love today.
As I move through all the different roles I play—
parent, child, student, worker, church member, supervisor, volunteer—
be my companion and strengthen my inner being
where I live with you. Amen.

Household Prayer: Evening

God of the embracing darkness,
thank you for dwelling in my heart.
I was able to accomplish some things today and not others.
Thank you for letting me rest in the promise
that you are able to accomplish abundantly more in my life
than all I can ask or imagine.
I will sleep in peace. Amen.

Proper 13

(Sunday between July 31 and August 6 inclusive)

SEMICONTINUOUS

2 Samuel 11:26–12:13a   Ephesians 4:1–16
Psalm 51:1–12   John 6:24–35

OPENING WORDS / CALL TO WORSHIP
We do not live by bread alone,
but by the Word who became flesh
and dwells among us.
Christ is the true bread of heaven,
the manna of freedom.
Come, let us worship and give thanks.

CALL TO CONFESSION
God has given us a sign
showing that love is stronger than death.
The sign of the cross
points to our exodus
from bondage to sin.
Let us repent,
seek God's forgiveness,
and enter into new life in Christ.

PRAYER OF CONFESSION
Holy One,
whose love and justice condemn us,
whose mercy and kindness feed us,
we confess our sins
and pray for your forgiveness.
What terrible suffering we have unleashed.
We have used other persons without regard for their dignity;
we have abused the earth without care for its beauty
or concern for future life;

we have sought to bargain with you
to smooth our way to heaven.
God, change us.
Put the Spirit of Christ within us
and cause us to grow into mature, faithful disciples
of the one who came from you
to save us from our sin.
Free us from captivity to our selfishness,
bind us to the whole body of Christ,
and let us bear witness to the truth
that your love holds everything together in perfect unity.
We pray in the name of our Savior, Jesus Christ. Amen.

DECLARATION OF FORGIVENESS

The bread of life God sends
is the offering of the only begotten Son.
Whoever comes in Jesus Christ   *John 6:35*
shall never be hungry;
whoever believes in him
shall never thirst.
Believe the gospel;
in Jesus Christ our sins are forgiven. **Amen.**

PRAYER OF THE DAY

Loving Trinity,
your justice is the working out
of your mercy and peace on earth.
Nourish us with the power of the Son,
and let us grow into his image and likeness.
Humble us in our self-conceits
so that we act not arrogantly
but with humility, patience, forbearance, and love.
Equip us for ministry on behalf of all
who cry out to you.
Help us to live lives worthy of the calling
to which you call us in Jesus Christ, our Lord. **Amen.**

PRAYER FOR ILLUMINATION

Creator of unity,
Body of peace,
Spirit of community,
bind us together around your Word
and send us out to do your justice,
show your mercy,
and embody your redeeming love,
glorifying you, Holy Trinity. Amen.

PRAYERS OF INTERCESSION

God of tears,
you are the giver of joy.
Hear us as we pray for the sick.
We pray for those with chronic illness,
for those who have life-threatening conditions,
and for those with inadequate medical care.
Bring the healing we need.
Hear us as we pray for all who are hungry.
We pray for those who live in regions of drought and famine,
for those who cannot afford nutritious food,
and for the vulnerable who are not adequately fed.
Give us the food we need.
Hear us as we pray for those who grieve.
We pray for those who mourn a loved one,
for those whose communities are no more,
and for those who cannot imagine a joyful future.
Give us comfort to restore hope.
Hear us as we pray for the world's victims.
We pray for those who are caught in violence,
for those who are trapped in others' self-seeking,
and for those who suffer from neglect.
Grant us freedom from all evil.
God of the poor and the poor in spirit,
we pray for your help against all that oppresses,
as we look forward to the kingdom you have promised
and are bringing even now through Jesus Christ,
in whose name we pray. **Amen.**

INVITATION TO THE OFFERING

The worship God blesses
is honest and personal,
a broken and contrite heart.   *Ps. 51:17b*
When we give of ourselves to God,
our hearts are changed for good.
Let us present tithes and offerings.

PRAYER OF THANKSGIVING/DEDICATION

O Trinity,
your love creates us,
your passion saves us from sin,
your power transfigures us into glory for you.
Thank you for giving us a place
in your good creation,
for giving us the bread of heaven
to free us from slavery to sin and death
and for filling us with the holy light of the gospel
for the building up of Christ's body in love.
We present offerings to praise you
and to help in the service of the church.
Accept them as outward signs
of our joyful discipleship
in the name of Jesus Christ the Lord. **Amen**.

CHARGE

Be open to the Holy Spirit's leading
and grow as a member of Christ's body.
Love with God's love,
be at peace within yourself,
make peace with others,
prepare for the coming kingdom.
Worship God and God alone,
Holy Three, Holy One,
forever and always.

BLESSING

God surround you with love;
Christ forgive you your sin;
Holy Spirit fill you with eternal life.

Question for Reflection

In what specific situation is God calling you to exercise humility, gentleness, patience, forbearance, and love?

Household Prayer: Morning

Holy, holy, holy Lord, God Almighty,
as it was in the beginning,
is now and ever shall be,
your love endures forever.
I am like the flower
that blooms in its season,
watered by the earth and morning dew.
You send the sun and rain,
morning, midday, and evening,
giving light and life.
Thank you for protection through the night;
thank you for your presence in the dawn.
Renew my strength this day
and let me love you
with all my heart and soul and might.
Bear with me as I bear my cross for Christ,
for I know that I will falter.
You remember that I am only dust,
but you have breathed your Spirit into me
and my face is renewed.
How can I show my gratitude?
Grant that I may be one with the mind of Christ,
loving my neighbor as myself
and giving as freely of myself
as you have given yourself to me.
Guide me today to serve in deep peace
wherever there is need for healing or hope.
Use me to show others
that you are the power
who transforms the world
and that you are the One
who saves sinners.

This day and this night,
in this life and in the life to come,
let me live in you to praise you,
God who is three, God who is one. Amen.

Household Prayer: Evening

The day has run its course,
evening lights are coming on,
and you are still with me, unseen, God.
You have been so quiet,
like the sun or misty rain
or the whisper of a light breeze across my skin.
Yet you gave me life today
to be in your presence,
and you gave me faith enough to hope
that I might be serving you.
You, who makes the universe
(or, if there are multiverses, so be it),
you, who turned a Roman weapon of torture and terror
into the ultimate sign of salvation,
you have been like a friend to me.
Thank you.
As I take moments to reflect on the day,
write in my journal, or pray even now,
I am sure there are ways you have cared for me
of which I am insensitive or unaware.
I am sure there are things I have done
and other things I failed to do
that made you justly angry with me.
I am sorry; please forgive me.
Do not let the darkness envelop me tonight.
Embrace me with your light
so that I can be at peace with you, restored.
Prepare me for tomorrow,
and for the day of resurrection,
when all creation will rejoice in your glory,
Holy Trinity. Amen.

Proper 13

(Sunday between July 31 and August 6 inclusive)

COMPLEMENTARY

Exodus 16:2–4, 9–15	Ephesians 4:1–16
Psalm 78:23–29	John 6:24–35

CALL TO WORSHIP / OPENING WORDS

Come, let us worship our God,   *Eph. 4:2, 4–6*

for there is one Lord, one faith, one baptism,

one God and Parent of all,

who is above all and through all and in all.

We come with humility, gentleness, and patience,

bearing with one another in love.

CALL TO CONFESSION

Let us confess our sin together,

for we have all fallen short of the glory of God.   *Rom. 3:23*

PRAYER OF CONFESSION

God, you have called us to live lives

worthy of the calling

to which we have been called.   *Eph. 4:1*

But we confess to you and each other

that we have not always spoken the truth in love;   *Eph. 4:15*

we have not always made every effort

to maintain the unity of the Spirit in the bond of peace.   *Eph. 4:3*

Forgive us and, by your grace,

help us to grow in every way

into him who is our head, Jesus Christ. Amen.   *Eph. 4:15*

DECLARATION OF FORGIVENESS

Sisters and brothers in Christ,   *Eph. 3:16–19*

the promise of our faith is that

whoever turns to Jesus Christ   *John 6:35*

will never hunger for forgiveness
and that which gives life to the world.
That is a promise of joy and of peace,
and I invite you to share that peace with one another.

PRAYER OF THE DAY

Giver of life,
every day you rain down manna from heaven
so that we can eat the bread of angels. *Ps. 78:25*
Turn our complaints into gratitude,
that we, as a church,
may mature into the body of the risen Christ *Eph. 4:13*
given for the life of the world. **Amen.**

PRAYER FOR ILLUMINATION

Holy God, may the reading of your Word *John 6:33*
be for us the bread you send from heaven
that gives life to the world. **Amen.**

PRAYERS OF INTERCESSION

God of love and liberation,
we give thanks for the stories of our faith
in which you fed Israel in the wilderness
and Jesus fed the hungry crowds that followed him.

Like them, we sometimes forget to be grateful for
what we have
and are consumed by complaining about what we
do not have.
Like them, we sometimes grab more than our
daily bread.
Help us to take only what we need and leave the rest
for those who hunger.

Forgive us when we follow Jesus or pray to you
only seeking after our own good.
Help us to pray for higher things,
for the things that will equip us for the work of ministry *Eph. 4:12*
and to perform the works of God. *John 6:28*

Holy One, we pray for this community,
for its families, its individuals, its children.
We pray for the nations of the earth,
that the world may know plenty and peace.
We pray for those who hunger for bread
and for those who hunger for righteousness,
that they will be fed what they need.

We pray in the name of Jesus Christ,
whom you sent to be bread for the world.
Giver of Life, give us this bread always. **Amen.**

INVITATION TO THE OFFERING
Each of us has been given grace   *Eph. 4:7*
according to the measure of Christ's gift.
Let us give a measure of what has already been
 given to us.

PRAYER OF THANKSGIVING/DEDICATION
Loving God, as you fed your people in the wilderness,
use our gifts, time, and talents as the manna
to meet the hungers of the world in which we live.
For Jesus' sake. **Amen.**

CHARGE
Equipped now for the work of ministry,   *Eph. 4:12*
go in peace and be bread for the life of the world.

BLESSING
May God,
Creator, Christ, and Holy Spirit,
fill you with all good things,
providing for you today and forever.

Questions for Reflection

In John 6:26–27, Jesus says that people were looking for him not because
they saw signs but because they had eaten their fill of the bread he had
multiplied. What do you think he meant? What is "the food that endures
for eternal life"?

Household Prayer: Morning

Holy One, as I move through this new day,
I pray that you will keep me in union
with the faith and knowledge of Jesus.
I long to mature into the stature of Christ.
Help me to speak the truth in love today,
that I may grow into him,
my savior, my teacher, and my friend, Jesus Christ. Amen.

Household Prayer: Evening

Thank you, God, for being my traveling companion today.
Instead of counting sheep as I fall asleep tonight,
help me to count all the forms that your manna took
as you fed me with the bread of life today.
Good night, God. I love you. Amen.

Proper 14

(Sunday between August 7 and August 13 inclusive)

SEMICONTINUOUS

2 Samuel 18:5–9, 15, 31–33   Ephesians 4:25–5:2
Psalm 130   John 6:35, 41–51

OPENING WORDS / CALL TO WORSHIP

By the power of the Holy Spirit   *Ps. 130:7; Eph. 4:30*
our steadfast loving God reaches out to redeem us.   *John 6:51*
Thanks be to God!

CALL TO CONFESSION

Let us confess our sins
to the One who hears our voice   *Ps. 130:2*
and is deeply moved by our distress.   *2 Sam. 18:33*

PRAYER OF CONFESSION

God of peace, we have rejected your redemption
    and forged our own way.   *2 Sam. 18:5–8*
We hang between heaven and earth, caught up
    in our own folly.   *2 Sam. 18:9*
We have held fast to falsehood, deceiving others
    and ourselves.   *Eph. 4:25*
We have sinned against you and done violence
    to others.   *2 Sam. 18:15*
Bitterness and wrath, anger and wrangling,
    slander and malice consume us.   *Eph. 4:31*
Evil runs rampant in our hearts.   *Eph. 4:27*
If you, O Lord, should mark our iniquities, Lord,
    who could stand?   *Ps. 130:3–6*
But there is forgiveness with you so that
    you may be revered.
Our soul waits in hope for your word to redeem us
so that we may begin anew, a new day with you. Amen.

DECLARATION OF FORGIVENESS

People of God, hope in the Lord! *Ps. 130:7*
God in Christ has forgiven you! *Eph. 4:32*
God has redeemed us from all our iniquities *Ps. 130:8*
through Christ, who loved us and gave himself for us *Eph. 5:2*
as living bread for the life of the world. *John 6:51*

PRAYER OF THE DAY

Redeeming God, *Ps. 130:7*
you satisfy our soul's hunger through Jesus Christ,
  the bread of life. *John 6:35*
Filled with your steadfast love, let us live in love, *Ps. 130:7; Eph. 5:2*
working honestly to share with the needy, *Eph. 4:28*
feeding others with the bread of kindness, *Eph. 4:32*
tenderness, and forgiveness. **Amen.**

PRAYER FOR ILLUMINATION

God of daybreak, *Ps. 130:5–6*
our souls wait for your light
more than those who watch for the morning.
Let your Holy Spirit illumine our hearts *Eph. 4:30*
with the light of your redemption,
a new day, a new life in Christ. **Amen.**

PRAYERS OF INTERCESSION

Let us pray for the needs of the world God so loves,
  saying,
We wait for you, Lord, in your word we hope.

Attentive God, we lift our voice to you. *Ps. 130:2*
Drawn by your steadfast love *Ps. 130:7; John 6:44*
and confident in your great power to redeem,
we pray for the church, those in need, and all
  your creation.
We wait for you, Lord, **in your word we hope.** *Ps. 130:5*

Bless your church to extend mercy to the outcast, *2 Sam. 18:5*
kindness to the stranger, and forgiveness
  to the erring. *Eph. 4:32*
We wait for you, Lord, **in your word we hope.**

Redeem your creation from the wilderness of
   sin and death   *2 Sam. 18:8;*
to the flourishing of righteousness and life.   *John 6:49*
We wait for you, Lord, **in your word we hope.**

Restore justice with mercy and truth with trust   *2 Sam. 18:5;*
in our nations and neighborhoods.   *Eph. 4:25–29*
We wait for you, Lord, **in your word we hope.**

Raise up those who cry from the depths   *Ps. 130:1*
of poverty, oppression, illness, and despair.
We wait for you, Lord, **in your word we hope.**

Help us to put away bitterness and wrath,
   anger and slander,   *Eph. 4:31*
and be kind to one another, living in love as you
   have loved us.   *Eph. 4:32; 5:2*
We wait for you, Lord, **in your word we hope.**

Let your love embrace those we now remember aloud
   and in our hearts.
[Names may be called forth from the assembly.]
We wait for you, Lord, **in your word we hope.**

Thank you for our ancestors, who ate your living bread
   and live forever.   *John 6:49–51*
We wait for you, Lord, **in your word we hope.**

Nourishing God, to you we commit our prayers   *John 6:35*
through Christ, the bread of life. **Amen.**   *John 6:48*

INVITATION TO THE OFFERING
Christ loved us and gave himself up for us.   *Eph. 5:1–2*
As beloved children, let us be imitators of God,
presenting our gifts as a fragrant offering
   and sacrifice,
through Christ our Lord.

PRAYER OF THANKSGIVING/DEDICATION

Generous, transforming God, *Eph. 4:28; 5:2*
thank you for the blessing of honest labor,
through which you have provided these gifts
for our hands to share with those in need.
We dedicate them now as an expression of your love
    for the world,
through Christ our Lord. **Amen.**

CHARGE

Drawn by the Father, nourished by Christ, *John 6:44, 35*
and sealed by the Holy Spirit, *Eph. 4:30*
go now to imitate God's love, *Eph. 5:1; 4:28, 32*
feeding the hungry, forgiving the hateful,
and spreading the fragrance of grace wherever
    there is need. *Eph. 5:2; 4:29*

BLESSING

God feeds us forever with the bread of life *John 6:35*
and upholds us with steadfast love. *Ps. 130:7*
You are blessed, redeemed, and gifted with grace
through Christ our Lord!

Questions for Reflection

"Put away from you all bitterness and wrath and anger and wrangling
and slander, together with all malice, and be kind to one another,
tenderhearted, forgiving one another, as God in Christ has forgiven
you" (Eph. 4:31–32). Have you ever experienced bitterness, wrath, anger,
wrangling, slander, or malice in yourself or from others? How do you
overcome and find grace to forgive?

Household Prayer: Morning

God of the morning watches,
my soul waits for you, and I hope in your word.
Bread of life,
nourish, strengthen, and accompany me throughout this day,
that I may labor honestly, share with the needy,
and imitate your love. Amen.

Household Prayer: Evening

God of peace, I have struggled through the battle of life this day.
If you should mark my iniquities, how can I stand?
But there is forgiveness with you.
Let your steadfast love cleanse, comfort,
and keep me through this night. Amen.

Proper 14

(Sunday between August 7 and August 13 inclusive)

COMPLEMENTARY

1 Kings 19:4–8	Ephesians 4:25–5:2
Psalm 34:1–8	John 6:35, 41–51

OPENING WORDS / CALL TO WORSHIP
I will bless the Lord at all times;   *Ps. 34:1, 3*
his praise shall continually be in my mouth.
O magnify the Lord with me,
and let us exalt God's name together.

CALL TO CONFESSION
Putting away falsehood, let all of us speak the truth
 to our neighbors,   *Eph. 4:25*
confessing our sins before God and one another.

PRAYER OF CONFESSION
Merciful God,
we confess that we have not lived as your
 faithful children.
We have been angry with the world   *Eph. 4:26–32*
and nursed grudges against our adversaries.
We have hoarded the fruits of our labors
rather than share our bounty with the needy.
We have not built up our neighbors with
 words of kindness
but have indulged in evil gossip.
We have not forgiven the wrongs others have done,
even though we desire your forgiveness toward us
 in Jesus Christ.
Heal us, O God,
and give us the grace to love
as Christ loved us and gave himself up for us. Amen. *Eph. 5:2*

DECLARATION OF FORGIVENESS

Let us put away bitterness and wrath and anger
    and wrangling and slander,   *Eph. 4:31–32*
together with all malice,
    and be kind to one another, tenderhearted,
forgiving one another, as God in Christ has forgiven us.
Thanks be to God.

PRAYER OF THE DAY

Eternal Father [God],   *John 6:35, 44*
your Son Jesus Christ is the true bread from heaven.
Draw us to Christ
that we may receive nourishing grace for our journey
    in this world
and know at last the joy of everlasting life with Christ,
who dwells with you and the Holy Spirit,
one God, forever and ever. **Amen.**

PRAYER FOR ILLUMINATION

Almighty God,
as we hear your gracious Word,
make us hungry for Jesus, your holy manna,
that we may feed on him,
the bread of life. **Amen.**   *John 6:51*

PRAYERS OF INTERCESSION

Sisters and brothers,
confident in God's love in Jesus Christ,
let us pray for the world and for our needs, saying,
Merciful God, hear our prayer.

God, you have called forth the church to embody
    your way of life.
Help those who profess faith in Christ to be
    faithful disciples
and live according to your Word.
For all who follow Jesus Christ,
Merciful God, **hear our prayer.**

Your children imitate you by speaking truth,
    showing forgiveness,   *Eph. 5:1–2*
and dwelling together in loving community.
For our neighbors and our neighborhoods,
that we may live in peace and justice,
Merciful God, **hear our prayer.**

God, our civic leaders face daily challenges
    and temptations.
For government officials,
that they may have integrity of heart
    and wisdom of judgment
    in their performance of public service,
Merciful God, **hear our prayer.**

God, the people of earth hunger for the spiritual food
    you provide
that gives meaning to life.
But many also hunger for good bread, for safe
    drinking water,
and for the bare necessities of life.
For those who struggle against the dehumanizing
    power of poverty,
and for those who pursue justice in the sharing
    of earth's resources,
Merciful God, **hear our prayer.**

God, your world is filled with the delights of natural beauty,
but also with danger of natural disaster.
For the planet Earth, our home,
that people may dwell in peace with the land,
honoring its beauty, conserving its resources,
and respecting its power,
Merciful God, **hear our prayer.**

Merciful God,
hear the prayers of your people
and grant that what we ask in faith
we may receive according to your gracious love,
through Jesus Christ, our Lord. **Amen.**

INVITATION TO THE OFFERING

As Christ loved us and gave himself up for us,   *Eph. 5:2*
let us offer ourselves to God.

PRAYER OF THANKSGIVING/DEDICATION

Receive these gifts, O God.
May our lives be a fragrant offering that is pleasing to you,   *Eph. 5:2*
in union with Christ's offering for us. **Amen.**

CHARGE

Church, we have received the bread of life.
Go forth to share this gift with others.
We go in Jesus' name.

BLESSING

May God, the source of life,
energize you with the Spirit, the power of life,
and fill you with Christ, the bread of life,
that you may receive eternal life.

Questions for Reflection

What do you hunger for in life? Do you hunger only for things you truly
need, or do you hunger for things you want but which may not be good for
you or for those around you?

Household Prayer: Morning

Loving God,
as I break the fast of evening rest
give me an appetite for your good gifts.
Let my hunger be satisfied
with the nourishing bread of life
you offer in Jesus Christ,
that I may receive strength for the journey this day holds. Amen.

Household Prayer: Evening

Lord Christ,
you are the bread that has sustained me.
Let me rest in peace,
trusting that the grace you have given me for this day
will be renewed like manna in the wilderness,
nourishment for the challenge of tomorrow
and confirmation of the promise of eternal life. Amen.

Proper 15

(Sunday between August 14 and August 20 inclusive)

SEMICONTINUOUS

1 Kings 2:10–12; 3:3–14   Ephesians 5:15–20
Psalm 111   John 6:51–58

OPENING WORDS / CALL TO WORSHIP

> The God of wisdom sent Jesus Christ,   *1 Kgs. 3:9;*
>   the bread of life,   *John 6:51*
> to teach us his ways, feed us with his   *Ps. 111:10;*
>   flesh and blood,   *John 6:54–56*
> and fill us with the Holy Spirit.   *Eph. 5:18*
> **Thanks be to God!**

CALL TO CONFESSION

> Let us confess our sins to the all-wise God
> who is gracious and merciful   *Ps. 111:4, 5*
> and keeps covenant with us.

PRAYER OF CONFESSION

> **All-knowing God, we are your children,**   *1 Kgs. 3:7, 11–14;*
> **but we have turned away from your wisdom**   *Eph. 5:16–18;*
> **and walked in our own ways.**   *Ps. 111:10*
> **We have lived carelessly and squandered time.**
> **We have been foolish and failed to understand**
>   **your will.**
> **We have been drunk with the wine of this world**
> **and debauched in our own desires.**
> **Purge us from evil and fill us with your Spirit.**
> **Clear our minds from clutter**
> **that we may discern what is right**
> **and walk in your ways. Amen.**

DECLARATION OF FORGIVENESS

The Lord is gracious and merciful!	*Ps. 111:4*
God shows great and steadfast love to us	*1 Kgs. 3:6*
through Jesus Christ, our bread of life.	*John 6:51*
By his flesh and blood our sins are forgiven	*John 6:54*
and we have eternal life. Alleluia! **Amen.**	*John 6:57*

PRAYER OF THE DAY

God our Living Father,	*John 6:57*
we give you thanks for sending our Lord Jesus Christ	*Eph. 5:20*
to give his life as bread for the world.	*John 6:51*
Fill us now with your Spirit	*Eph. 5:18*
that we may make the most of the time,	*Eph. 5:16*
understanding your will and expressing your wisdom	*Eph. 5:15, 17*
in the midst of the people you have chosen. **Amen.**	*1 Kgs. 3:8–9*

PRAYER FOR ILLUMINATION

Great God of steadfast love,	*1 Kgs. 3:6*
we study your works and delight in your ways.	*Ps. 111:2*
Illumine our understanding by your Holy Spirit,	*Eph. 5:18*
that we may reverence your name, grow in your wisdom,	*Ps. 111:10*
and discern between good and evil. **Amen.**	*1 Kgs. 3:9*

PRAYERS OF INTERCESSION

Let us pray to God, saying,
You have redeemed your people. Holy and awesome
   is your name.

Faithful God, you are ever mindful of your covenant	*Ps. 111:5, 8*
and invite us to ask gifts of your goodness.	*1 Kgs. 3:5*
In your steadfast love, receive our requests	*1 Kgs. 3:6*
for the well-being of your church, your world,	
and your people.	
You have redeemed your people.	
Holy and awesome is your name.	*Ps. 111:9*

Grant your church understanding and discernment
to faithfully carry out your mission in the world.
You have redeemed your people.
Holy and awesome is your name.

Cause us to walk in wisdom concerning
    your creation,
mindfully stewarding its provision for all
    living creatures.
You have redeemed your people.
    Holy and awesome is your name.

Give those who govern wise and discerning minds,   *1 Kgs. 3:9–12*
that your way of justice and compassion may prevail
    among the nations.   *Ps. 111:6*
You have redeemed your people.
    Holy and awesome is your name.

Provide food for the hungry, hope for the despairing,   *Ps. 111:5*
and wisdom for the wandering.
You have redeemed your people.
    Holy and awesome is your name.

Help us make the most of the time,   *Eph. 5:16*
walking in your ways, filled with your Spirit,   *1 Kgs. 3:14;*
    living out your will.   *Eph. 5:17–18*
You have redeemed your people.
    Holy and awesome is your name.

In your steadfast love, let your wisdom uphold   *1 Kgs. 3:6, 9*
those we remember now aloud and in our hearts.
[Names may be called forth from the assembly.]
You have redeemed your people.
    Holy and awesome is your name.

We give you thanks for our ancestors, the great people
    you have chosen   *1 Kgs. 3:8*
in all generations, who now rest with you.   *1 Kgs. 2:10*
You have redeemed your people.
    Holy and awesome is your name.

Holy and awesome God, you are the answer to
    our prayers;
through Christ our Lord. **Amen.**

INVITATION TO THE OFFERING

Christ, our living bread, has given his flesh for the life
of the world. *John 6:51*
Filled with the Spirit, let us offer our gifts of
thanksgiving to God *Eph. 5:18, 20*
through our Lord Jesus Christ.

PRAYER OF THANKSGIVING/DEDICATION

We give thanks to you, God, *Eph. 5:20*
for sending your Son Jesus to be living bread
for the world. *John 6:57*
Breathe on these gifts we bring,
that through them your life may feed, strengthen,
and bless this world, *Ps. 111:5*
through Christ, our bread of life. **Amen.** *John 6:51*

CHARGE

Be filled with the Spirit and make the most
of the time. *Eph. 5:16, 18*
Walk in wisdom and grow in understanding *1 Kgs. 3:14;*
of God's will, *Eph. 5:17*
feeding on the flesh and blood of Jesus Christ, *John 6:54–56*
our living bread. *John 6:51*

BLESSING

The God of steadfast love feeds you *1 Kgs. 3:6*
with the flesh and blood of Jesus Christ, *John 6:54–56*
fills you with the Spirit, *Eph. 5:18*
and guides you with wisdom; *1 Kgs. 3:12*
in the name of the Father and of the Son
and of the Holy Spirit.

Question for Reflection

"At Gibeon the LORD appeared to Solomon in a dream by night; and God
said, 'Ask what I should give you'" (1 Kgs. 3:5). If God said to you, "Ask
what I should give you," how would you respond?

Household Prayer: Morning

I praise you, Lord, and give you thanks for the gift of this new day.
Fill me with your Holy Spirit. Let your songs fill my heart.
Give me a wise and discerning mind to walk in your way,
making the most of the time as I go out among your people. Amen.

Household Prayer: Evening

Gracious and merciful God,
I have gone out and come in today seeking to do your will,
yet there is so much that I do not understand or discern.
I commit to you my questions, concerns, and anxieties.
Grant me peaceful sleep
as I rest in your wisdom and steadfast love. Amen.

Proper 15

(Sunday between August 14 and August 20 inclusive)

COMPLEMENTARY

Proverbs 9:1–6	Ephesians 5:15–20
Psalm 34:9–14	John 6:51–58

OPENING WORDS / CALL TO WORSHIP
Come, O children, listen to me;   *Ps. 34:11, 14*
I will teach you the fear of the Lord.
Depart from evil, and do good;
seek peace, and pursue it.

CALL TO CONFESSION
Seeking the wisdom of the Lord,   *Eph. 5:15–16*
let us consider how we have lived,
confessing our sins
and trusting in the mercy of God.

PRAYER OF CONFESSION
Merciful God,
we confess that we have not been faithful children.
We have not lived by your law;
we have remained silent in the face of evil;   *Ps. 34:13–14*
we have not refrained from deceit;
we have not followed in the way of peace;
and we have not honored all that is true and good.
We have been foolish and immature people   *Eph. 5:17*
who resist the holy wisdom you graciously offer.   *Prov. 9:6*
Forgive us our sin, O God,
and lead us to sincere repentance
through Jesus Christ. Amen.

DECLARATION OF FORGIVENESS
Hear the good news:
Christ offers himself as bread of life

to all who would receive him.
This proves his love for us.
In the name of Jesus Christ, you are forgiven.
Thanks be to God.

PRAYER OF THE DAY

Eternal Father [God], *John 6:51*
your Son Jesus Christ is the true bread from heaven.
Help those who receive his body and blood
to be the body of Christ for the world,
sharing the riches of his grace
with all who hunger and thirst for eternal life;
through Christ who dwells with you and the Holy Spirit,
one God, forever and ever. **Amen.**

PRAYER FOR ILLUMINATION

Almighty God, through the reading of holy Scripture,
feed us with your living Word
and reveal to us the way of everlasting life. **Amen.**

PRAYERS OF INTERCESSION

Sisters and brothers,
as Christ offered himself for the life of the world,
let us pray for the needs of the world, saying,
Merciful God, hear our prayer.

God, we pray for the church in every land:
confirm in the hearts of Jesus' disciples
a will to serve you by loving their neighbors
and doing good to their enemies.
For the church catholic,
Merciful God, **hear our prayer.**

God, we pray for those who lead your church:
guide the bishops, pastors, elders, deacons, teachers,
      and administrators
who order the life of Christian community,
and strengthen them to be faithful in their calling
      and humble in service.
For *[bishop N., pastors N. and N., etc.]*

and those who lead the churches throughout the world,
Merciful God, **hear our prayer.**

God, we pray for those who govern the nations and
    exercise authority in civic life:
give our governing officials wisdom in the ways
    of peace and justice
and a determination to pursue the common good.
For President *[name]*, for Governor *[name]*, for our mayor,
and the rulers of every nation and city,
Merciful God, **hear our prayer.**

God, we pray for the sick, the poor, and the oppressed:
help those who are in trouble
and stir up in your church a desire to be your instruments
in the relief of human misery.
For those in need,
Merciful God, **hear our prayer.**

God, we pray for our planet Earth:
calm the storm and quiet the rumbling volcano;
give us seasonable weather and tranquil seas.
Let Earth yield an abundance of fruit
for the flourishing of every creature,
and give humankind the will to use its resources wisely.
For the good earth,
Merciful God, **hear our prayer.**

Merciful God,
hear the prayers of your people
and grant that what we ask in faith
we may receive according to your gracious love,
through Jesus Christ, our Lord. **Amen.**

INVITATION TO THE OFFERING
God has given to us the bread of life.
With joyful hearts, let us offer ourselves and
    our gifts to God.

PRAYER OF THANKSGIVING/DEDICATION

Receive, O God, the fruits of our labor
and with these gifts accept the offering of our lives.
Unite us with Christ
that we may share in his ministry and glorify you. **Amen.**

CHARGE

Church, go forth to love and serve.
We go in Jesus' name.

BLESSING

The blessing of God, source of life,
the grace of Christ, bread of life,
and the communion of the Spirit, power of life,
be with you.

Question for Reflection

What does Jesus mean when he says his body is "true food" and his blood
is "true drink" (John 6:55)?

Household Prayer: Morning

Loving God,
help me make the most of the time you give this day,
to be wise in my decisions
and careful in my actions.
Let my life be a continual act of thanksgiving
for your loving-kindness,
through Jesus Christ. Amen.

Household Prayer: Evening

Loving God,
if I have not lived wisely this day,
show me my foolish ways.
Fill me with the Spirit
that I may know your will and live by your truth,
for I long to be your faithful child
and to abide eternally with Jesus Christ, your Son. Amen.

Proper 16

(Sunday between August 21 and August 27 inclusive)

SEMICONTINUOUS

1 Kings 8:(1, 6, 10–11)	Ephesians 6:10–20
22–30, 41–43	John 6:56–69
Psalm 84	

OPENING WORDS / CALL TO WORSHIP

The living God has sent the living bread   *Ps. 84:2, 5, 7;*
    from heaven   *John 6:57–58*
to fill our hearts with strength!   *Eph. 6:10*
In the name of the Father and of the Son and
    of the Holy Spirit. **Amen.**

CALL TO CONFESSION

Let us confess our sins
to the One whose eyes are open day and night   *1 Kgs. 8:28–30*
to heed our cry and our prayer.

PRAYER OF CONFESSION

Watchful God, you know our plight.   *1 Kgs. 8:29; John 6:64*
Offended, we have not believed your words.   *John 6:60–61, 64*
Complaining, we have betrayed your love.
We are weak, estranged, wandering, and lost.   *John 6:66*
Seeking to stand in our own strength, we fall.   *Eph. 6:10–11*
Strangers to your holiness, we wander.   *John 6:69*
Defenseless against evil within and without,
    we are lost.   *Eph. 6:13*
Shine your light in our darkness,   *Ps. 84:11*
and guide us back to our place in you. Amen.   *Ps. 84:4–5*

DECLARATION OF FORGIVENESS

The Living God hears our cry and forgives our sin!   *1 Kgs. 8:30*
The Lord God is a sun and shield, bestowing favor
    and honor on us   *Ps. 84:11*

through Christ, the bread from heaven,   *John 6:58*
who brings us back to God and feeds us
        with his strength.   *John 6:56–57, 63*

PRAYER OF THE DAY
God our strength, you have brought us into
        your holy place   *1 Kgs. 8:6, 10–11;*
through Christ, who has the words of eternal life.   *John 6:63, 68*
As you made us alive by his flesh and blood,   *John 6:56–58*
cause us to boldly witness to the gospel,   *Eph. 6:15, 19–20*
welcome the stranger, and pursue peace,   *1 Kgs. 8:41–43; Eph. 6:15*
standing through the struggles of our times.
    Amen.   *Eph. 6:10–14*

PRAYER FOR ILLUMINATION
Holy God, you have the words of eternal life.   *John 6:68*
By your Holy Spirit, let your words pierce
        our darkness,   *Eph. 6:17*
strengthen our faith, and illumine our witness   *Ps. 84:9;*
        for you. **Amen.**   *Eph. 6:16, 19–20*

PRAYERS OF INTERCESSION
Let us pray to the Lord, saying,
O God, keep your promise. You have the
        words of life.

Faithful God, there is no one like you in heaven
        or on earth.   *1 Kgs. 8:23–27*
The highest heaven cannot contain you,
yet you dwell in our midst and regard our prayers   *1 Kgs. 8:28–30;*
        with favor.   *Ps. 84:9–11*
So we lift our hearts in your house, praying by the   *1 Kgs. 8:22;*
        power of your Spirit   *Eph. 6:18*
and persevering in supplication for the church,   *1 Kgs. 8:22*
        the creation, and those in need.
O God, keep your promise.   *1 Kgs. 8:25–26;*
    You have the words of life.   *John 6:68*

Let your church stand firm in the strength
    of your power,   *Eph. 6:10–20*
overcoming evil and proclaiming the gospel of peace.
O God, keep your promise.
    You have the words of life.

Bless us to care for your creation, the sanctuary
    you have provided   *Ps. 84:3*
to nourish, sustain, and shelter humankind
    and all living things.
O God, keep your promise.
    You have the words of life.

May the rulers, authorities, and cosmic powers
    of this present darkness   *Eph. 6:12*
yield to your reign of love, peace, justice,
    and goodness for all.
O God, keep your promise.
    You have the words of life.

Protect and comfort the weak, the young;   *Ps. 84:3*
Hear the cry of the stranger, the forgotten.   *1 Kgs. 8:41–43;*
O God, keep your promise.   *Ps. 84:3*
    You have the words of life.

Strengthen our faith, deepen our love, empower   *John 6:64;*
    our witness.   *Eph. 6:14–17*
O God, keep your promise.
    You have the words of life.

May those we remember now find refuge in the
    midst of your mercy.   *Ps. 84*
[Names may be called forth from the assembly.]
O God, keep your promise.
    You have the words of life.

Happy are those who have passed into your presence
    in hope of the resurrection.   *Ps. 84:4–7*
O God, keep your promise.
    You have the words of life.

Lord God, you are our sun and shield, our strength
   and hope.   *Ps. 84:11*
With joy, we entrust our prayers to you through
   Jesus Christ our Lord. **Amen.**   *Ps. 84:12*

INVITATION TO THE OFFERING

Our God has bestowed us with favor and honor   *Ps. 84:11*
through Christ, who has given us the words
   of eternal life.   *John 6:68*
From this fullness, let us now offer our gifts
   of thanksgiving
in the name of Jesus Christ, our Savior and Lord.

PRAYER OF THANKSGIVING/DEDICATION

Living God, we give you thanks for Christ, the bread
   from heaven,   *John 6:58*
through whom we offer these gifts.
Endow these gifts with your power,
that they may express your steadfast love
and impart your sustaining strength to all those
   in need. **Amen.**

CHARGE

Be strong in the Lord and in the strength
   of God's power.   *Eph. 6:10*
Put on the whole armor of God so that you may
   be able to stand firm   *Eph. 6:11, 13*
as you boldly proclaim the gospel of peace
   in word and deed.   *Eph. 6:15, 19–20*

BLESSING

The living God gives you strength!   *Ps. 84:5–7*
The Lord Jesus Christ feeds you with his flesh
   and blood!   *John 6:56–58*
The Holy Spirit fills you with life!   *John 6:63*
You are blessed by the Holy Trinity!

Questions for Reflection

"Likewise when a foreigner, who is not of your people Israel, comes from a distant land because of your name . . . and prays toward this house, then hear in heaven your dwelling place, and do according to all that the foreigner calls to you" (1 Kgs. 8:41–43). Are there people of other nationalities, ethnic groups, or faith traditions in your workplace, neighborhood, community, or congregation? What are some ways in which you and your congregation can express the welcome of God to those who are different from you?

Household Prayer: Morning

Lord God, my sun and shield,
a day in your courts is better than a thousand elsewhere.
Let the favor of your presence strengthen me and accompany me
everywhere I go today.
Prepare me to be a sanctuary,
that your light and love may radiate through me.
Through Christ my Lord. Amen.

Household Prayer: Evening

Lord God my strength, your Spirit never tires; your love never fails.
I bring you my struggles, stresses, questions, and worries of this day.
Where else can I go? You have the words of eternal life.
Let your promises sustain my soul and comfort my heart as I rest in you,
through Christ my Lord. Amen.

Proper 16

(Sunday between August 21 and August 27 inclusive)

COMPLEMENTARY

Joshua 24:1–2a, 14–18   Ephesians 6:10–20
Psalm 34:15–22   John 6:56–69

OPENING WORDS / CALL TO WORSHIP
The Lord redeems the life of his servants.   *Ps. 34:22*
Thanks be to God!
No one who takes refuge in him will be condemned.
Praise the Lord!

CALL TO CONFESSION
Because God is near to the brokenhearted,   *Ps. 34:18*
let us consider how we have lived,
  confessing our sins
and trusting in God's mercy to save.

PRAYER OF CONFESSION
God of our redemption,
we confess that we have not been faithful servants.
We have not served you with sincere hearts   *Josh. 24:14–18*
nor trusted in your salvation.
We have forsaken you, the living God,
and have chosen to follow the lifeless idols
of worldly power and wealth.
Forgive us our sin, O God.
Lead us to heartfelt repentance
that we may honor you with our lips
and serve you with our lives;
through our Savior, Jesus Christ. Amen.

DECLARATION OF FORGIVENESS
Hear the good news:
Christ himself is the Word that offers eternal life   *John 6:68*
to all who receive him. This proves his love for us.
In the name of Jesus Christ, you are forgiven.
Thanks be to God.

PRAYER OF THE DAY
Living God,
your Son Jesus Christ has the words of eternal life.
Grant that we may come to him in faith,   *John 6:65*
follow him in this world,
and abide with him forever in the world to come;
for he dwells with you and the Holy Spirit,
one God, forever and ever. **Amen.**

PRAYER FOR ILLUMINATION
Lord Jesus Christ,
as we hear the reading of Holy Scripture,
speak to us your words of spirit and life. **Amen.**   *John 6:63*

PRAYERS OF INTERCESSION
Sisters and brothers,
as Christ offered himself for the life of the world,
let us pray for the needs of the world, saying,
Merciful God, hear our prayer.

God, we pray for the church in every land:
Help all who serve the living God to be strong in the
    power of God   *Eph. 6:10–11*
and to withstand all the temptations of the evil one.
For the church universal,
Merciful God, **hear our prayer.**

God, we pray for those who lead your church:
Guide the bishops, pastors, elders, deacons, teachers,
    and administrators
who order the life of Christian community,
that they may persevere in supplication for
    all the saints   *Eph. 6:18–19*

and make known with boldness the mystery
of the gospel.
For *[bishop N., pastors N. and N., etc.]*
and those who lead the churches throughout the world,
Merciful God, **hear our prayer.**

God, we pray for those who govern the nations and
exercise authority in civic life:
Give our governing officials wisdom for the
administration of justice,
compassion for the sake of mercy,
and determination for the pursuit of the common good.
For President *[name]*, for Governor *[name]*, for our mayor,
and for the rulers of every nation and city,
Merciful God, **hear our prayer.**

God, we pray for the sick, the poor, and the oppressed:
Save those who are in need
and strengthen all who minister to them.
For those in trouble or want,
Merciful God, **hear our prayer.**

God, we pray for our planet Earth:
Save our world from the ravages of war,
thoughtless waste, and the foolish exploitation
of Earth's abundance.
For the good earth,
Merciful God, **hear our prayer.**

Merciful God,
hear the prayers of your people
and grant that what we ask in faith
we may receive according to your gracious love,
through Jesus Christ, our Lord. **Amen.**

INVITATION TO THE OFFERING

Let all who revere the Lord, *Josh. 24:14*
who desire to serve the Lord in sincerity and
in faithfulness,
bring their gifts with joyful hearts.

PRAYER OF THANKSGIVING/DEDICATION

Almighty God,
we dedicate ourselves to serve you,
for you alone are our God.   *Josh. 24:18*
Receive, O God, the gifts we offer,
and with these gifts accept the offering of our lives;
through Christ in the power of the Holy Spirit. **Amen.**

CHARGE

Sisters and brothers,
you have chosen to serve God
because God has chosen you in Jesus Christ.
Go, therefore, to love and serve as God's people in the world.
We go in Jesus' name.

BLESSING

The blessing of God, who delivers us,
the grace of Christ, who sustains us,
and the communion of the Spirit, who empowers us,
be with you always.

Questions for Reflection

In the Gospel of John, Peter declares to Jesus, "You have the words of
eternal life. We have come to believe and know that you are the Holy One
of God" (John 6:68–69). Are "believing" and "knowing" the same action?
How does knowing something intensify our believing something?

Household Prayer: Morning

Living God,
give me strength for this day.
Let your truth surround me,
your righteousness defend me,
your gospel guide me,
your trustworthiness shield me,
and your salvation protect me,
that in every trial I may stand by the power of your Spirit
and live by your holy Word. Amen.

Household Prayer: Evening

Loving God,
as the day ends and the night begins
be near the brokenhearted,
save the crushed in spirit,
and redeem the life of your servants.
You are our shield by day.
Be our refuge by night
so that we may rest in the confidence of your grace;
through Christ our Lord. Amen.

Proper 17

(Sunday between August 28 and September 3 inclusive)

SEMICONTINUOUS

Song of Solomon 2:8–13	James 1:17–27
Psalm 45:1–2, 6–9	Mark 7:1–8, 14–15, 21–23

OPENING WORDS / CALL TO WORSHIP

God has lavished us with every perfect gift *Jas. 1:17;*
   from above *Song 2:10*
and called us to living intimacy through the
   beloved one, Jesus Christ our Lord.

CALL TO CONFESSION

Let us confess our sins
to our loving God who calls us close *Song 2:10*
through our beloved Savior, Jesus Christ our Lord.

PRAYER OF CONFESSION

Loving, righteous God, *Ps. 45:7*
our hearts are defiled with the wickedness *Mark 7:15,*
   you hate. *21–23*
You have called us to yourself, but we have *Song 2:10;*
   gone away. *Jas. 1:24*
Forgetting your living Word, we cling to *Mark 7:3–5;*
   dead traditions. *Jas. 1:22–24*
Deceiving ourselves, we abandon *Mark 7:8;*
   your commandments. *Jas. 1:22*
Hypocrites, we honor you with our lips *Mark 7:6*
while our hearts are far from you.
Cleanse our hearts from evil intentions; *Mark 7:21–23; Jas. 1:21*
cleanse our tongues from evil words *Jas. 1:26*
so that our worship may be pure and undefiled *Jas. 1:27*
and we may live with you in love for others. Amen.

DECLARATION OF FORGIVENESS

Our generous God has given us the perfect gift
    of forgiveness, *Jas. 1:17*
Jesus Christ our Lord,
who has liberated us from dead tradition *Jas. 1:25, 27*
and made us new by the living Word, *Jas. 1:18*
filling our hearts with God's love.

PRAYER OF THE DAY

Unchanging God, you have blessed us forever *Ps. 45:2, 6*
through the Beloved One, Jesus Christ our Lord. *Song 2:8–9*
Born again by your word of truth, *Jas. 1:18*
let us live out your love, doing your word, *Jas. 1:25*
caring for the weak and vulnerable in their distress, *Jas. 1:27*
and ever pursuing your reign of justice, *Ps. 45:6*
through Jesus Christ our Lord. **Amen.**

PRAYER FOR ILLUMINATION

Father of lights, there is no variation or shadow
    due to change in you. *Jas. 1:17*
Let your Spirit illumine our hearts through
    your holy Word,
turning us from the emptiness of our human traditions *Mark 7:7–8*
to the fullness of life in the Beloved One, Jesus Christ
    our Lord. **Amen.** *Song 2:8–13*

PRAYERS OF INTERCESSION

Let us bring our prayers of intercession to God, saying,
Arise, God of Love. Come to our aid.

Beloved One, you have called us to your embrace *Song 2:8–10*
and our hearts overflow with your goodness. *Ps. 45:1*
Your power endures forever. *Ps. 45:6–7*
You reign with justice and love righteousness.
Let the fragrance of your love and the grace
    on your lips *Ps. 45:2, 8*
anoint us now as we pray for the church, the creation,
    and all those in need. *Ps. 45:7*
Arise, God of Love. **Come to our aid.** *Song 2:8–10*

Unshackle your church from bondage to
    human tradition   *Mark 7:7–8*
that we may worship you freely and serve others
    with a pure heart.   *Jas. 1:27*
Arise, God of Love. **Come to our aid.**

Redeem and renew your creation to bud, blossom,
    and bring forth fruit   *Song 2:11–13*
as we care for the land and love one another.
Arise, God of Love. **Come to our aid.**

Extend your reign of compassionate justice in
    our nations and neighborhoods   *Ps. 45:6*
as we unite with people of goodwill to do right
    for those in need.   *Ps. 45:7; Jas. 1:27*
Arise, God of Love. **Come to our aid.**

Let us embrace the distressed, the diseased,
    the devalued, the denied.   *Jas. 1:27*
Cause us to care for the abandoned, the bereaved,
    the weak, and the weary.
Arise, God of Love. **Come to our aid.**

Make us be quick to listen, slow to speak, slow to anger.   *Jas. 1:19*
Let us persevere in your perfect law of liberty and
    bless us to do your Word.   *Jas. 1:25*
Arise, God of Love. **Come to our aid.**

Clothe those we remember now
with your fragrant grace and renewing love.   *Ps. 45:2, 8;*
[Names may be called forth from the assembly.]   *Song 2:11–13*
Arise, God of Love. **Come to our aid.**

Blessed forever are those who have answered
    your invitation: *Ps. 45:2*
"Arise, my love, my fair one, and come away."   *Song 2:10*
They now rest in your embrace.
Bless us now to follow in their footsteps of faith.
Arise, God of Love. **Come to our aid.**

Anointed with your oil of gladness,   *Ps. 45:7*
let our prayers rise as fragrant incense before you
through Jesus Christ our Lord. **Amen.**

INVITATION TO THE OFFERING

Every generous act of giving, with every perfect gift,   *Jas. 1:17*
is from above, coming down from the Father of lights.
Filled by God's generosity, let us offer our gifts
    with gladness
through Jesus Christ our Lord.

PRAYER OF THANKSGIVING/DEDICATION

Living God, thank you for your gifts of life—
fragrant flowers, fruitful vines, singing creatures,   *Song 2:12–13*
and our own lives, renewed in Christ.   *Jas. 1:18*
Let your grace infuse the gifts we offer
with life-giving power for those in need.
In the name of the Father and of the Son and
    of the Holy Spirit. **Amen.**

CHARGE

Listen to the life-giving words of the Beloved One,
    Jesus Christ our Lord!   *Mark 7:14*
Look into God's perfect law of liberty and persevere
    in God's blessing!   *Ps. 45:2; Jas. 1:25*
Live in God's love, caring for those in need from
    a heart filled and blessed   *Jas. 1:27*
by the power of the Holy Spirit through Jesus Christ
    our Lord.

BLESSING

God has blessed you forever with every perfect gift   *Ps. 45:2;*
    from above,   *Jas. 1:17*
freeing you to rise and live in the embrace
    of God's love.   *Song 2:10*

Questions for Reflection

"My beloved speaks and says to me, 'Arise, my love, my fair one, and come away'" (Song 2:10). Song of Solomon portrays a vivid picture of romantic love in poetic form. Can you recall an experience of romantic love? In what ways does romantic love parallel our relationship with Christ? In what ways is it different?

Household Prayer: Morning

Beloved Savior, my heart overflows with your goodness.
The night has passed. The morning has come.
Your voice calls me to arise and come with you into this new day.
Let your love strengthen me to answer your call and follow you,
caring for those in need of your love. Amen.

Household Prayer: Evening

Christ, Beloved One, I desired to keep pace with your
    steps of love today,
but I found my mind wandering, my feet straying,
    my heart forgetting your love.
Gather me again in your gracious embrace
    and renew my strength
as I rest in your love this night. Amen.

Proper 17

(Sunday between August 28 and September 3 inclusive)

COMPLEMENTARY

Deuteronomy 4:1–2, 6–9   James 1:17–27
Psalm 15   Mark 7:1–8, 14–15, 21–23

OPENING WORDS / CALL TO WORSHIP
Who may abide in the presence of God?   *Ps. 15:1–2*
Who may live on God's holy mountain?
All those who walk blamelessly and do what is right.
All those who speak truth from their heart.

CALL TO CONFESSION
With sincere hearts and minds,
let us confess our sins before God and the world,
trusting in God's mercy to forgive.

PRAYER OF CONFESSION
God of light,
we confess that we live in the shadows of hypocrisy
and self-righteousness.   *Jas. 1:17*
We honor you with our lips, but we have not
served you in our hearts.   *Mark 7:6*
We are satisfied with human traditions and norms   *Mark 7:7–8*
and avoid your liberating truth.

We have confused meekness with weakness,
holiness with social conformity,
and anger with righteousness.   *Jas. 1:19–20*
Forgive us, we pray.
By the power of your word
save us from the prison of our conceit   *Jas. 1:20*
so that we may serve you with sincere hearts;
through Jesus Christ, our Lord. Amen.

DECLARATION OF FORGIVENESS

Friends, do not despair:
God renews us by the word of truth,   *Jas. 1:18*
that we might become the first fruits of God's creation.
In the name of Jesus Christ, we are forgiven.

PRAYER OF THE DAY

Almighty God, in Jesus Christ
you have shown us the truth of your commandments.
Give us sincere hearts
that we may serve you with joy,
obey you with love,
and manifest your wisdom to the world;   *Deut. 4:6*
through Christ and by the power of the Holy Spirit. **Amen.**

PRAYER FOR ILLUMINATION

Lord, by the power of your Spirit
open our hearts and minds to receive your Word
that we not forget the wonders you have done   *Deut. 4:9*
nor neglect to make them known to our children,
nor fail to tell them to the world. **Amen.**

PRAYERS OF INTERCESSION

*[Silence is kept after each response to allow the
congregation to offer intercessions.]*
In peace, let us pray to God, saying,
God of light, hear our prayer.

For the church of Jesus Christ,
God of light, **hear our prayer.** *[brief silence]*
Bless the church, O God.
Deliver us from self-righteousness
and make us holy in every way,
that all people may see you
in the witness of your faithful servants.

For our pastors, teachers, and ministers,
God of light, **hear our prayer.** *[brief silence]*

Bless the leaders of your church, O God,
[our bishop N., our presiding elder N., our pastors N.,]
and all who minister in your name.
Give them the wisdom to discern your truth,
to honor your commandments,
and to lead with humility.
Let them walk blamelessly, do what is right,   *Ps. 15:2*
and speak truth from their heart.

For the world and for its leaders,
God of light, **hear our prayer.** *[brief silence]*
Bless the nations of the world, O God.
Guide the leaders of governments for the sake of peace.
Give them sound judgment and merciful hearts
and help them be accountable for the common good.
Save them from the cynicism of war.
Free them from the influence of greed.
Deliver them from the temptations of social power.

For the community in which we live,
God of light, **hear our prayer.** *[brief silence]*
Bless our communities, O God.
Help us live as friends with our neighbors
and do good to one another,
that homes may be free of fear
and families live in peace.

For children,
God of light, **hear our prayer.** *[brief silence]*
Bless children and those who care for them, O God.
Project them from harm;
give them what they need to grow in body and mind
and provide caring adults to model for them a life of
    purpose and compassion.

For the sick and those in distress,
God of light, **hear our prayer.** *[brief silence]*
Bless all who are ailing in body, mind, or spirit.
Heal them of their disease and restore them to fullness of life.

For those who are judged by others,
God of light, **hear our prayer.** *[brief silence]*
Bless those who face the reproach of society, O God:
those in prison, whether innocent or guilty of crimes;
those who are ostracized due to mental disease,
whether or not they pose a threat to others;
those who are homeless, and those who are lost to addiction.
Surround them with compassion and save them from hopelessness.

These prayers we offer to you, God of light,
through Christ, by the power of your Holy Spirit. **Amen.**

INVITATION TO THE OFFERING

Let us give as God has so abundantly given to us.

PRAYER OF THANKSGIVING/DEDICATION

O God, receive these gifts for the work of your church.
With these gifts we dedicate ourselves
to live in the truth of your word,
and follow your commandments
with sincere hearts;
through Christ our Lord. **Amen.**

CHARGE

Go in peace to love and serve.
We go in the name of Christ.

BLESSING

The blessing of God be with you,
the love of Jesus fill you,
and the power of the Holy Spirit sustain you,
now and forevermore.

Questions for Reflection

How can we know the difference between human tradition and the commandments of God? How can we know that we serve God from the heart?

Household Prayer: Morning

Lord Jesus,
help me walk blamelessly and do what is right,
to speak the truth in love,
to avoid gossip and slander,
and do good to all I meet,
that I may abide in your presence
and dwell in fellowship with the Holy Trinity. Amen.

Household Prayer: Evening

Lord, you have been my light this day.
As evening comes, be my light in the darkness.
With meekness I welcome the word you have implanted in my heart,
and with confidence I claim the power of salvation
in Jesus Christ.
And let me rest from my labors,
confident that in you there is no shadow of fear. Amen.

Proper 18

(Sunday between September 4 and September 10 inclusive)

SEMICONTINUOUS

Proverbs 22:1–2, 8–9, 22–23	James 2:1–10 (11–13), 14–17
Psalm 125	Mark 7:24–37

OPENING WORDS / CALL TO WORSHIP

Our merciful God, maker of us all,	*Prov. 22:2; Jas. 2:13*
pleads the cause of the poor and afflicted.	*Prov. 22:22–23*
Open our hearts to demonstrate God's grace	*Mark 7:34–35*
through Jesus Christ our Lord.	

CALL TO CONFESSION

Let us confess our sins	
to the Lord who surrounds us with favor	
forevermore.	*Ps. 125:2; Prov. 22:1*

PRAYER OF CONFESSION

God of favor, we have not been true to you.	*Prov. 22:1; Jas. 2:1*
You have chosen the poor in the world,	
but we have dishonored them.	*Jas. 2:5–6*
You plead the cause of the afflicted,	
but we crush them.	*Prov. 22:22–23*
We have not loved our neighbors as ourselves.	*Jas. 2:8*
We have favored the rich and despised the poor.	*Jas. 2:1, 9*
We have dismissed the needy with empty words.	*Jas. 2:15–17*
Soften our hearts and make straight our ways.	*Ps. 125:5*
Heal our unbelief and turn us back to you. Amen.	

DECLARATION OF FORGIVENESS

The mercy of our God triumphs over judgment	*Jas. 2:12*
through our glorious Lord Jesus Christ,	*Jas. 2:1*
who has pleaded our cause, forgiven our sin,	*Prov. 22:23*
healed our sickness, and delivered us from evil.	*Mark 7:24–37*

PRAYER OF THE DAY

Good and generous God,	*Ps. 125:4; Prov. 22:9*
you have blessed us with favor and counted us	*Ps. 125:2;*
as your people	*Prov. 22:1*
through our glorious Lord Jesus Christ.	*Jas. 2:1*
Freed by your grace, let us extend your generosity	*Prov. 22:9;*
to others,	*Mark 7:24–35*
sharing our bread with the poor, pleading the	*Prov. 22:9;*
cause of the afflicted,	*Jas. 2:15–17*
and receiving all who assemble in your name	*Jas. 2:2–5*
with the warmth of your love and the richness	
of your hospitality;	*Jas. 2:8*
in the good name of Jesus Christ,	*Prov. 22:1;*
our Savior and Lord. **Amen.**	*Jas. 2:7*

PRAYER FOR ILLUMINATION

Healing God, you do all things well.	*Mark 7:34–35, 37*
Illumine our hearts by your Holy Spirit,	
that we may receive your words and demonstrate	
your grace. **Amen.**	

PRAYERS OF INTERCESSION

Let us pray to the God of mercy, through our savior,
   Jesus Christ, saying,
O Lord, plead our cause. Your name is good.

God our maker,	*Prov. 22:2*
you surround your people with favor	
and goodness.	*Ps. 125:2; Prov. 22:1*
You have chosen the poor in the world	
to be rich in faith	*Jas. 2:5*
and to inherit your promised kingdom	
through our Lord Jesus Christ,	
who heals the afflicted and sets the oppressed free.	*Mark 7:24–37*
In your mercy, open our mouths in intercession	
as we bow at your feet	*Mark 7:25, 34–35*
on behalf of the church, the creation, and	
all those in need.	
O Lord, plead our cause. **Your name is good.**	*Prov. 22:1, 23; Jas. 2:7*

Open your church to welcome and honor the poor,   *Jas. 2:1–8*
meeting their needs with faith-filled deeds of love
    and generosity.   *Jas. 2:14–16*
O Lord, plead our cause. **Your name is good.**

Uphold the land and those who labor to cultivate it,
that both crops and people may be sustained
    by your love
and overflow with the blessings of your
    generous provision.
O Lord, plead our cause. **Your name is good.**

Establish justice for the poor, relief for   *Ps. 125:3;*
    the afflicted,   *Prov. 22:23*
and compassionate care for the physically
    and mentally ill.   *Mark 7:24–37*
O Lord, plead our cause. **Your name is good.**

May we respect the dignity of all who struggle,   *Jas. 2:1–8*
showing your kindness to those in need.   *Jas. 2:14–17*
O Lord, plead our cause. **Your name is good.**

Open our ears to hear the cry of the poor.   *Mark 7:32–35*
Open our mouths to advocate for the afflicted.   *Mark 7:35*
Open our hands to lift up those who are
    pressed down.   *Mark 7:28–30*
Open our hearts to share generously with
    those who lack,   *Prov. 22:9*
especially those we remember now aloud
    and in our hearts.
[Names may be called forth from the assembly.]
O Lord, plead our cause. **Your name is good.**

Bless the faithful poor and afflicted
who have passed into your presence today
to receive the rich inheritance you have prepared
    for them
in your kingdom.   *Jas. 2:5*
O Lord, plead our cause. **Your name is good.**

We trust in you to do us good   *Ps. 125:4*
through the excellent name of Jesus Christ,   *Jas. 2:7*
our Savior and Lord. **Amen.**

INVITATION TO THE OFFERING

Those who are generous are blessed   *Prov. 22:1, 9;*
through the good name of Jesus Christ our Savior,   *Jas. 2:7*
by whom we have received the favor of our God—
    better than silver or gold.
From the riches of God's grace,
let us present our gifts of gratitude to bless those in need.

PRAYER OF THANKSGIVING/DEDICATION

Generous God, thank you for these gifts   *Prov. 22:9*
we bring from your abundance.
Bless gifts and givers to show your love to all those
    in need   *Jas. 2:8*
through our glorious Lord Jesus Christ,   *Jas. 2:1*
healer of the sick, advocate of the afflicted,   *Prov. 22:23;*
provider for the poor. **Amen.**   *Mark 7:24–37*

CHARGE

Favored by the excellent name of Jesus Christ
    our Savior and Lord,   *Prov. 22:1; Jas. 2:7*
share your bread with the poor, advocate
    for the afflicted,   *Prov. 22:9, 22–23*
show your faith in acts of kindness, love your
    neighbor as yourself.   *Jas. 2:8, 14–17*

BLESSING

Our generous God has blessed us   *Prov. 22:9*
and surrounded us with favor forever,   *Ps. 125:2*
that we may love our neighbors as ourselves   *Jas. 2:8, 14–17*
through the good name of Jesus Christ, our Savior
    and Lord.   *Prov. 22:1; Jas. 2:7*

Questions for Reflection

"Listen, my beloved brothers and sisters. Has not God chosen the poor in the world to be rich in faith and to be heirs of the kingdom that he has promised to those who love him? But you have dishonored the poor" (Jas. 2:5–6a). A UNICEF study reports that the United States has the second-highest child poverty rate in the industrialized world, with more than one in five children living in households that fall below the poverty line (http://www.unicef-irc.org/publications/pdf/rc10_eng.pdf). What does this mean to you as a person of faith? How might God call the church to respond to this situation?

Household Prayer: Morning

Generous God, you are my maker and I trust in you.
Surround me with your favor today
that I may hear the cry of those in need
and share my resources with the poor;
in the excellent name of Jesus Christ, my Savior and Lord. Amen.

Household Prayer: Evening

Good and constant God, I have endeavored to love my neighbor
    as myself today.
Yet the needs are so great that I find my heart failing and
    my faith falling short.
In your mercy, let the favor of Christ surround me with strength.
Restore me as I rest in you. Amen.

Proper 18

(Sunday between September 4 and September 10 inclusive)

COMPLEMENTARY

Isaiah 35:4–7a	James 2:1–10 (11–13), 14–17
Psalm 146	Mark 7:24–37

OPENING WORDS / CALL TO WORSHIP
Here at the feast of God's holy word and holy meal,
eyes and ears are opened so that we may all
be made glad and filled with hope.

CALL TO CONFESSION
Many people brought their greatest needs to Jesus,
certain that he would help them.
With that same confidence, let us confess our failings
and seek forgiveness.

PRAYER OF CONFESSION
Almighty and compassionate God,
every day, in our desire to
attain our wants,
avoid discomfort,
and shun those we do not know or love,
we show ourselves to be unworthy of your gifts of life.
Of this we are sorely aware,
and we ask your power to renew us in body and spirit,
that we will be able, through your help,
to walk in the way you intend for us.
Forgive us and lead us, in Jesus' name. Amen.

DECLARATION OF FORGIVENESS
Just as Jesus made the deaf to hear and the mute to speak,   *Mark 7:37*
our merciful God lifts our burdens from us,
removes the failures of our past,
and turns us to new life.

You are forgiven.
Walk in peace.

PRAYER OF THE DAY
God of love,
you show your people how to be truly rich in faith,
through the gifts you give when least hoped for or expected.
Come to your people today with words of both judgment and mercy,
that we may be fed from the bread of life.
We pray this in your holy triune name: Father, Son, and Holy Spirit,
one God, Mother of us all. **Amen.**

PRAYER FOR ILLUMINATION
Holy God, whose Spirit comes to us
in moments of both strength and weakness,
come now into our midst that we might be able to hear your Word
in fullness and in truth, through Jesus Christ, our Lord. **Amen.**

PRAYERS OF INTERCESSION
Confident that God hears us and knows our needs, let us pray
for all creation, saying,
Hear us, O God, for your mercy is great.

Gracious healer, you visit us when we are in pain and worry.
You spread your hands on our wounds.
You speak to demons.
You bring peace and freedom.
Visit your churches and synagogues, mosques and ashrams,
monastic cells and places of prayer in every land
for the well-being of all people of faith. Make us one.
Hear us, O God, **for your mercy is great.**

Creator of beauty and surprising complexity,
we long for the wisdom we need in order to cherish this earth.
Give us the vision to see what you have made—
vast expanses of prairie, forests dark and thick,
oceans full of wondrous creatures,
and the heavens bigger than our imaginations.
Show us how to keep your gifts as good stewards.
Hear us, O God, **for your mercy is great.**

Liberator of the captive,
you know the failings of the nations
when we turn our friends and neighbors into enemies.
Free our lands from despotic rulers, tricksters,
people who lie for personal gain, and those who wield hate speech.
Give courage and perseverance to those
who are weary of the struggles for justice
so that new life and strength will infuse their tired bones.
Hear us, O God, **for your mercy is great**.

Savior, we see the desperation of our sisters and brothers
as well as ourselves,
and knowing your love for what you have made,
we beg your promises to be fulfilled:
waters in the desert,
healing even in the time of death,
protection from whatever is frightening,
salvation for those who are without help.
Hear us, O God, **for your mercy is great**.

Holy God, we pray for those who grow our food
and keep our water clean,
for politicians who make good laws
and judges who rule with compassion,
for children, for elders, for parents and grandparents,
aunts, uncles, and friends and strangers.
Give to your world the means to live in harmony.
Hear us, O God, **for your mercy is great**.

Almighty one, you heard the cry of the Syrophoenician woman
and you answered her distress with a word.
Say the word again today and relieve the suffering of your people.
We pray especially for *[name those in the assembly's care]*
and those we name now aloud or in our hearts. *[silence]*
Hear us, O God, **for your mercy is great**.

For those who have helped us know you, we give you thanks.
Hear us, O God, **for your mercy is great**.

Into your hands we place the welfare of all creation,
in the name of the one whose life, death, resurrection,
and ascension is our own life, Christ Jesus. **Amen.**

INVITATION TO THE OFFERING

For the healing of this world,
let us now bring forth our tithes and offerings.

PRAYER OF THANKSGIVING/DEDICATION

Receive our thanks, O God,
for your gifts of life, means, and time.
We treasure your offerings and, small as our return giving may be,
welcome it for the sake of those in need
and for the furtherance of your witness in this world.
Make us daily more grateful for all we have been given,
in Jesus' name. **Amen.**

CHARGE

Be strong and do not fear!   *Isa. 35:4*
Trust in the Lord's blessings of answered prayer
    and healing.
Listen to the wisdom around you.
Speak well of your neighbors.
Teach peace.

BLESSING

May the God who made you, loved you, and lives with you,
bring you to a faith that cannot be weighted down
and a courage that knows no bounds.

Questions for Reflection

Try to recall the first time in your life when you did not retreat in the face
of opposition. How is your experience like that of the Syrophoenician
woman putting her case to Jesus? Where in your life today is that same
courage calling you to speak out? What could you do this week to take
steps in that direction?

Household Prayer: Morning

Holy God, I thank you for another day,
whether it brings the sort of happiness for which I always hope
or the challenges I sometimes fear.
Each day in your presence is a time
to notice the marvels of creation that surround me.
Help me to see them today
and to move gracefully from one hour to the next,
in the name of your holy and miraculous ways. Amen.

Household Prayer: Evening

Giver of all good things,
you have been at my side, beneath, above, and within me all day long,
and I thank you for your presence.
I thank you now, as well, that as I grow weary,
you have given me a place to lay my head.
Watch over all who sleep this night,
especially those who have no shelter.
Guard them and keep all your people in safety, in Jesus' name. Amen.

Proper 19

(Sunday between September 11 and September 17 inclusive)

SEMICONTINUOUS

Proverbs 1:20–33	James 3:1–12
Psalm 19	Mark 8:27–38

OPENING WORDS / CALL TO WORSHIP

Look at the heavens!   *Ps. 19:1–4, 14*
They are shouting the glory of God.
The days and the nights declare the magnificence
of God's creative works.
Their voice goes through all the earth
and their words reach the ends of the world.
Let our words of praise be acceptable to you.
Our Lord, our rock, our redeemer!

CALL TO CONFESSION

Let us use our voices to declare those things we have
    said and done
that have separated us from God, and from
    each other,
that we may experience God's mercy and receive
    God's forgiveness.

PRAYER OF CONFESSION

You have called us, O God,   *Jer. 23:25–29*
and we have refused to listen;
you have stretched out your hand
and we have not taken it.
We have taken what you have given us
and used those gifts to hurt others and defy you.
We have refused to be tamed by your wisdom.
Forgive our inability to recognize you
and live out the reality of your gospel.

**Give us the insight we need
to understand your place in our lives
so that our words and actions reflect
the glory of God in the lives of others.
In the name of the Messiah we pray. Amen.**

DECLARATION OF FORGIVENESS

The law of the Lord is perfect,   *Ps. 19:7–8*
and it revives the soul;
the decrees of the Lord are sure
and make wise the simple;
the precepts of the Lord are right,
rejoicing the heart;
the commandment of the Lord is clear,
and it enlightens the eyes.
Hear the good news!
In Jesus Christ, the living Word,
we are forgiven. Live in peace!

PRAYER OF THE DAY

It says in the Bible, O God,
that you created the world
through your Word.
Your Word is powerful!
And so are our words.
They can heal, create a smile,
be a declaration of love;
but they can also hurt
and destroy a sense of self-worth.
Give us your wisdom, God of the Word,
so that as a church and as individuals,
we use our words to build up
and not to destroy. **Amen.**

PRAYER FOR ILLUMINATION

Let the words of our mouths   *Ps. 19:14*
and the meditations of our hearts
be acceptable to you, O Lord.
Be our Rock and our Redeemer. **Amen.**

PRAYERS OF INTERCESSION

God of love, you gave your only Son
so that he would undergo great suffering for our sake.
Seeing this great suffering,
we believe that you understand
the sufferings of the world
and our own suffering.
Believing that you have walked
in our footsteps and that you have lived through
trials and tribulations,
we offer our prayers to you.

We pray for wisdom,
that we can communicate effectively
with love, shalom, and compassion
and strive to live in connectedness
and understanding.

We pray for courage
so that we can live out our faith
giving witness with our words and actions
that you are the Messiah.

We pray for the will
to take up the cross and to follow
wherever you may lead.

And we pray for love,
your love in us
so that we can live with the intentionality
to know each other by name
and have the deep relationships
that you want us to have with you
and with each other.
Through Jesus Christ,
who lives in unity with you
and the Holy Spirit,
one God, forever and ever. **Amen.**

INVITATION TO THE OFFERING

God has given us the sun
and made us stewards of all creation.
God has given us our lives and our very beings.
Let us give to God, from what God has given us.

PRAYER OF THANKSGIVING/DEDICATION

God of wisdom,
may this offering serve
as a powerful witness
to this world in need.
Guide us as we administer
the gifts that you have given us
for the building of your kingdom.
In Jesus Christ we pray. **Amen.**

CHARGE

When people ask, Who is this Jesus?   *Mark 8:27–38*
do not be ashamed of the gospel;
share with them that he loved the world so much
that he lived for us, suffered for us, died for us,
    and rose again for us,
and invite them to follow him.

BLESSING

May God, our Wisdom, pour out God's   *Heb. 11:29–12:2;*
    thoughts in you   *Luke 12:49–56*
and make God's words known to you.
May Jesus Christ, our Messiah,
give you the strength to carry your cross and
    to follow him.
And may the Holy Spirit, our Tongue of fire,
guide our words and our actions,
as we strive to bless the world with our witness.

Questions for Reflection

How do you seek God's wisdom in your life? What are the signs and
symbols of God's presence that surround your everyday life?

Household Prayer: Morning

As I open my eyes,
I can see the heavens that tell of your glory.
Allow me to be part of this creation
that proclaims your handiwork
and your real presence in the world. Amen.

Household Prayer: Evening

As the day winds down,
allow me to find satisfaction in the thought
that I have taken my cross and followed you.
Allow me to find rest in the knowledge
that I did not act as if I was ashamed of you.
And if I failed you, forgive me
and allow me to find solace
in the new mercies of the morning. Amen.

Proper 19

COMPLEMENTARY

Isaiah 50:4–9a   James 3:1–12
Psalm 116:1–9 *or*   Mark 8:27–38
   Wisdom of Solomon 7:26–8:1

OPENING WORDS / CALL TO WORSHIP

Gracious is the Lord, and righteous;   *Ps. 116:5, 9*
our God is full of compassion.
Let us walk in the presence of the Lord
in the land of the living,
through Jesus Christ, our Savior.

CALL TO CONFESSION

The Lord listens to the cries of the people
who turn with full hearts to the One who has mercy.
Let our tongues now make confession in the presence of God
and of this body.

PRAYER OF CONFESSION

Holy God,
in the face of sin, our gravest enemy,
we call to you for help.
You know our fault before we speak.
Forgive us for what we have done in opposition to your will.
Forgive us for those things we have not undertaken
and for which we know our wrong.
We have not loved you and our neighbors as we ought.
We have denied our dependence on you.
Lead us away from this grief and sorrow.
Save us so that we may fulfill our vows to you
and attend to the needs of your people. Amen.

DECLARATION OF FORGIVENESS

God, who is gracious and merciful, knows the human desire
to save our lives by avoiding Jesus' call to carry the cross.
God, who is full of compassion, also knows that those who repent
have set their minds and hearts on what endures for all time.
Your sin is forgiven you.
The Lord God is a very present help
to those who seek to follow in the way of divine things.
Go with God in joy as you take up your cross, in Jesus' name.

PRAYER OF THE DAY

God of love,
you teach us a life journey that calls us to deny
what is unhealthy and unloving.
Lead us in that pathway.
Awaken us to the ever-new abundance
that is ours through your Word,
in the name of the one who died and rose,
Christ Jesus, our Lord, who lives and reigns
with you and the Holy Spirit, now and forever. **Amen.**

PRAYER FOR ILLUMINATION

You speak to us, Lord, with tongues of wisdom.
Let your Holy Spirit now open us to hear
with greater clarity the teachings of today,
that we may hold dear in yet new ways
what it is you will for us, in Jesus' name. **Amen.**

PRAYERS OF INTERCESSION

Let us pray for the church, the nations,
and all people seeking God's mercy and care, saying,
God of love, hear our prayer.

We pray for the church in every place,
that wherever people gather in your name,
you make us able to listen to each other with open hearts.
Give your people unity, O God,
and replace divisiveness with reconciliation.
God of love, **hear our prayer.**

We pray for all who serve the church
as musicians, ushers, greeters, pastors, council members,
teachers, and student leaders, as architects and cooks,
as repairers and cleaners, and in all other ministries.
God of love, **hear our prayer.**

We pray for Muslims and Jews, Hindus and Buddhists,
people of indigenous religions everywhere,
that their paths may lead—with ours—to greater understanding
of the goodness of faith in its many languages and forms.
God of love, **hear our prayer.**

We thank you for this amazing earth, for clean water,
rich soils, abundant sunshine, and all the foods that you have made
for our health and enjoyment.
Give all people the gratitude to share,
especially with those who do not have such riches
and who today are hungry.
God of love, **hear our prayer.**

We pray for the leaders of our nation . . .
for our president and members of Congress,
for the leaders asserting power in other nations,
for nations in trouble at this time
[name those where there is violence or disaster],
and for peacemakers and diplomats
as they work to shape a reformed people.
God of love, **hear our prayer.**

We pray for all who suffer from the horrors of war and famine,
for children who do not know the reason for their pain
and have no power to change their lot,
and for the animals and plants damaged by human conflicts.
God of love, **hear our prayer.**

We pray for those suffering from all forms of injustice, brokenness,
    or illness,
especially all who have asked for the prayers of this congregation
and for those whose well-being we hold in our hearts,
named now aloud or silently. *[silence]*
God of love, **hear our prayer.**

God of eternity, certain days remind us of tragedy and death,
but we know that all days are redeemed and held in your grace.
We remember those who have died on this day,
those who will die today,
and all whose lives have enriched ours
*[name here those whose memory is dear to the church catholic
or the local congregation]*.
Keep alive in us the hope of the resurrection.
God of love, **hear our prayer.**

Into your hands we commend those for whom we pray,
trusting in your mercy through your Son, Jesus Christ, our Lord.
    Amen.

INVITATION TO THE OFFERING
In the face of adversity,
the prophet Isaiah calls to the people:
Let us stand up together.   *Isa. 50:8*
This is a call to us, as well,
to stand together with our offerings,
given for the well-being of the church
and of those in need.
We will receive them now.

PRAYER OF THANKSGIVING/DEDICATION
Lord, who gives us everything we have,
we return with joy a portion of our bounty,
giving to the work of your church and your world
what is already yours: ourselves, our lives, and our means.
Make good come from these gifts.
Teach us to use what we have with wisdom and compassion.
In the name of Jesus we pray. **Amen.**

CHARGE
Take up your cross and follow Jesus.
Do not be afraid of what may come.
You lose what you wish to safeguard
only by holding onto it with too great a desperation.
Set your mind on what Christ Jesus has done.

May the teachings of your Creator, Redeemer, and Sustainer,
and the presence of the one God who abides with you always,
keep you strong and gentle,
for the sake of the goodness that is willed for you,
in Jesus' name.

Questions for Reflection

When we hear Jesus say we are to "deny" ourselves, this can seem strangely harsh language, and it is well that each of us knows what it means in our own lives. You are made in God's image. As an image of the divine, God does not command you to be nothing. You are not to be denigrated. What aspects of your life, your desires, your tendencies, do you recognize as impeding your ability to set your mind on what you truly want and need? What is your cross? Perhaps you see more than one cross you must bear. If you "take up" your cross (or crosses), how might you live differently than you do now?

Household Prayer: Morning

Thank you, God, for this good night and day,
for time to sleep and wake,
for dark and light,
for silence and noise,
for stillness and movement,
for my body, mind, and heart.
Give me the strength today to bear my cross with patience
so that whoever I meet will find a moment of calm
in my presence because of you.
I pray this in Jesus' name. Amen.

Household Prayer: Evening

Thank you, God, for this good day and now for night,
for all that has transpired in the last hours,
for the food I have been given,
for the work I have had to do,
for the exercise, for breathing, for what my ears have heard,

for friends, for coworkers,
and for what I have seen growing in the soil
and shining in the sunlight.
Guard me now as I sleep and give me good rest
for the sake of the tasks you have set before me tomorrow.
I pray for your peace, in Jesus' name. Amen.

Proper 20

(Sunday between September 18 and September 24 inclusive)

SEMICONTINUOUS

Proverbs 31:10–31   James 3:13–4:3, 7–8a
Psalm 1   Mark 9:30–37

OPENING WORDS / CALL TO WORSHIP

Happy are the people   *Ps. 1:1–2, 6*
who do not follow the advice of the wicked
or take the path that they follow,
or sit in the seat of people who make fun of others.
Their delight is in the law of the Lord,
and they meditate on God's law day and night.
The Lord watches over the way of the righteous,
but the way of the wicked will perish.

CALL TO CONFESSION

Recognizing that we are easily swayed
by the wrong advice
and that we have strayed from the ways of the Lord,
let us confess our sins to God,
with hope of finding love and mercy.

PRAYER OF CONFESSION

God of wisdom,   *Jas. 3:18*
forgive our foolishness.
We desire what we do not need
and corrupt our relationships with envy.
You urge us to gentleness,
but we stir up conflict.
Give us your grace,
that we may harvest righteousness and peace,
for the sake of Jesus Christ, our Teacher, we pray. Amen.

DECLARATION OF FORGIVENESS

Charm is deceitful and beauty is vain, *Prov. 31:30*
but the people who fear the Lord are to be praised.
Hear the good news!
In Jesus Christ we are forgiven and we can live
   in peace.

PRAYER OF THE DAY

God of the first and the last, *Mark 9:30–37*
give us strength of mind,
that we might walk the path of obedience
   and discipleship
without wasting our time thinking about who is
   more important.
Instead, guide our thoughts and our emotions
that we may be like children, totally dependent
   on you,
welcoming all with hospitality and love.
In the name of Jesus we pray. **Amen.**

PRAYER FOR ILLUMINATION

Your Word is our wisdom;
it gives us insight, strength, and courage.
Open our hearts and our minds on this day,
that we might receive what you want to give.
Speak, Lord! Your people listen! **Amen.**

PRAYERS OF INTERCESSION

[A time of silence follows each petition.]
God of understanding,
through the Word read and proclaimed,
and through your Word incarnate, Jesus Christ,
you give us the direction we need
and show us that there is nowhere else to go but to you
with our joys and our concerns.

We pray for our world that too often follows
the advice of wickedness that leads to war, to violence,
to conflict between ethnicities, to fear.

We pray for the women in this world
who, as payment for their devotion and love
as capable wives, daughters, sisters, girlfriends, mothers,
receive rejection, abuse, heartbreak, and hate.

We pray for relationships that are broken
by conflicts and dispute, by murder and deceit,
and that cannot find a way back to restoration and healing.

We pray for our children
who have been called the first
in God's heart and kingdom
but are not welcomed, loved, heard, or spoken to.

We believe in you, God of justice and mercy,
and we ask, trusting in your power,
to heal the wounded hearts,
to restore the brokenness of the world,
and to lead us to everlasting peace. **Amen.**

INVITATION TO THE OFFERING
We have been made capable
of being good stewards of what God has given us.
Let us, with gratitude in our hearts,
give from what has been given to us, by grace.

PRAYER OF THANKSGIVING/DEDICATION
Our great Gardener,   *Ps. 1:3*
we are like trees
planted by streams of water
that yield their fruit in season
and prosper in you.
We are grateful for all that you have provided,
and we dedicate our firstfruits to you
and to the work of your church,
now and forever. **Amen.**

CHARGE

Go out into the world   *Mark 9:30–37;*
endeavoring to be the last of all and the servant of all.   *Jas. 4:7–8a*
Welcome the children, for in doing so,
you welcome Jesus.
Submit yourselves to God,
resist all evil;
draw near to God,
and God will draw near to you.

BLESSING

May God, who watches over all the righteous,
give you the gifts needed to be a capable servant.
May Jesus Christ, who welcomes everyone,
give you the loving heart of a child
so that you can welcome others unconditionally.
May the Holy Spirit, who gives us the understanding
    we need
to love God and to love others,
give us unselfish and generous hearts,
to heal relationships and to live in peace.

Question for Reflection

What can you do to discern between good advice and advice that will lead
you on the wrong path?

Household Prayer: Morning

As we rise,
we have so much to do!
We work without realizing
that all we do can be a song of love to you
and to the ones with whom you have surrounded us.
Lead me, O God,
so that everything that I do in my life
can be done in praise to you. Amen.

Household Prayer: Evening

As this day ends,
I hope I have done my work
with a gentleness born out of your wisdom.
Thank you, triune God,
for the rest that you will provide
and for the strength for a new morning. Amen.

Proper 20

(Sunday between September 18 and September 24 inclusive)

COMPLEMENTARY

Wisdom of Solomon 1:16–2:1, 12–22	James 3:13–4:3,
or Jeremiah 11:18–20	7–8a
Psalm 54	Mark 9:30–37

OPENING WORDS / CALL TO WORSHIP
Little children, the one who welcomes you
is here in word and bread and wine.
Little children, young and old, all the baptized:
welcome to the place of hope.
Little children, Jesus calls us all into the circle of his arms. Come.
Thanks be to God.

CALL TO CONFESSION
Let us give up boasting and dishonesty,
turning to the Lord with our confessions,
because the one who knows us through and through
has promised to renew us.

PRAYER OF CONFESSION
O God, who makes known to us all truth,
we confess that we are weighed down by our failings:
envy distances us from other people;
greed alerts us only to our own desires.
Where we might bring reconciliation, we create conflicts.
Where you call us to give, we take.
Where your presence beckons, we resist.
Deal with us not as we deserve, O God,
but forgive us, cleanse us, and teach us your way. Amen.

DECLARATION OF FORGIVENESS

The God who loves and sustains you hears your plea.
The Lord desires for you a welcome
into the blessed community of freedom and light.
You are forgiven.
Remember the poor and the outcast,
welcome the child,
and you will know, as well, your own welcome,
in the name of the Father, Son, and Holy Spirit,
one God, Mother of all things, now and forever.

PRAYER OF THE DAY

Gentle Jesus, you call us to live in your name
with honor and respect,
fully known to you and precious in your sight.
Draw us near to you each day
as you teach us how to feed on your gifts,
through Jesus Christ, our Savior and Lord. **Amen.**

PRAYER FOR ILLUMINATION

We pray for your great wisdom, O God,
to come to your people and set us free.
Help us hear what the Spirit is saying to the church this day. **Amen.**

PRAYERS OF INTERCESSION

[A brief silence is kept after each petition.]
Let us pray for the church, the world, and all Earth's needs, saying:
God of mercy, hear our prayer.

We give you thanks, Holy One, for all that sustains life.
We thank you—
for good soil and clean air . . .
for the waters of Earth and especially *[name local waterways
and bodies of water]* . . .
for fish and mammals, birds and insects, for trees and plants
of every kind . . .
for all the varieties of people you have made and the richness
of our many cultures . . .
for responsible leaders and citizens, healthy nations, schools,
and plenteous food . . .
for shelter, clothing, medical care, and art . . .

for all those things we name now in gratitude, silently
    or aloud . . .
God of mercy, **hear our prayer.**

Almighty and gracious God, we call on your help
in the face of all that we do not know how to change. We pray—
    for people of faith everywhere . . .
    for the healing of Earth wherever there are scars . . .
    for all nations at war . . .
    for peacemakers, diplomats, and inventors . . .
    for families lacking the necessities of life . . .
    for people who are suffering in any way . . .
    for all those needs we lift before you now silently or aloud . . .
God of mercy, **hear our prayer.**

We lean on your compassion, O God,
and trust your promise to heed the cries of your people
and answer our need, in the name of your Son, Christ Jesus,
who lives and reigns with you and the Holy Spirit,
now and forever. **Amen.**

INVITATION TO THE OFFERING
Like the child Jesus held, we live and move and have our being
inside the circle of his arms.
Let us open our hearts so that our tithes and offerings
bring others, as well, into that circle.

PRAYER OF THANKSGIVING/DEDICATION
We thank you for the wealth you shower on us daily, O Lord,
and we witness the marvelous goodness that comes from you.
Transform these gifts into signs of welcome
for all who are touched by their use.
Transform us into people who bless others throughout each day,
in Jesus' name we pray. **Amen.**

CHARGE
For those who make peace,
a harvest of righteousness is sown.   *Jas. 3:18*
Be gentle, honest, and merciful with those you meet;
ask for wisdom,
and wisdom will fill you with joy.

BLESSING

The God of all creation,
who calls you to the power greater than death,
the Spirit of kindness and abundant life,
be with you now and always.

Question for Reflection

Give yourself some moments each day in the coming week to sit quietly
with your eyes closed. Visualize Jesus kneeling down, opening his arms,
and bringing you close to his heart. Let yourself be a little child who is
welcomed. What do you notice?

Household Prayer: Morning

Gracious God, you give life and, in your Word, it is beautiful.
Thank you for this new day.
In each coming hour, help me to see beneath
the ever-present difficulties and superficial joys
into the mysteries that you have set out for your people.
Guide me toward those I meet today
in a way that welcomes them and, in turn,
grants me a welcome, in Jesus' name. Amen.

Household Prayer: Evening

This day is nearly over, Merciful God, and I am tired.
I have been unable to do all that I had hoped;
I have done some things I would take back if I could.
Forgive me for my failures.
Bring me into the warmth and security of your embrace now,
and fill me with new vision
so that I may rest and rise to meet tomorrow with vigor,
in the name of Christ Jesus, our Lord. Amen.

Proper 21

(Sunday between September 25 and October 1 inclusive)

SEMICONTINUOUS

Esther 7:1–6, 9–10; 9:20–22   James 5:13–20
Psalm 124   Mark 9:38–50

OPENING WORDS / CALL TO WORSHIP

If it had not been for God, who was on our side,   *Ps. 124:1–8*
we would have fallen prey to those who want to
    harm us;
we would have been swept away by sadness and fear.
Blessed be the Lord, our protector!
God has broken the snare that took away our
    freedom.
Our help is in the name of the Lord,
who made heaven and earth.
Blessed be God's holy name!

CALL TO CONFESSION

The prayer of faith will save the sick,   *Jas. 5:15–16a*
and the Lord will raise them up,
and anyone who has committed sins
will be forgiven.
Therefore confess your sins to one another
and pray for one another
so that you may be healed.

PRAYER OF CONFESSION

God of unity,   *Mark 9:38–50*
we live in a world where our lives move
between inclusivity and exclusivity.
We often move toward the latter,
trying to oust from our circles
those who do not think like us,

181

act like us,
or look like us.
Forgive our need to reject
and to always be on the lookout
for those things that make us different.
Give us the eyes of our Teacher,
who knows unconditional love and compassion
and sees us all as one,
for it is in his name that we pray. Amen.

DECLARATION OF FORGIVENESS

My brothers and my sisters,   *Jas. 5:19–20*
if anyone among you wanders
from the truth and is brought back by another,
you should know that whoever brings back a sinner
     from wandering
will save the sinner's soul from death and will cover
     a multitude of sins.
Rejoice! You have been brought back
by the redemption of God
and forgiveness through Jesus Christ our Savior.
You can live in peace.

PRAYER OF THE DAY

God of courage,   *Esth. 7:3;*
you gave Esther the strength to speak out   *Mark 9:30–37*
and the intelligence she needed to save her people.
Help us to believe
that you are still present and active
in this world
and that your grace remains
as an everlasting force in our lives.
In Jesus Christ we pray. **Amen.**

PRAYER FOR ILLUMINATION

Your Word is our salt;
without it, we lose our being,
our joy, and our ability to endure.
Open our hearts and our minds
to listen, to really listen,
to your Word today. **Amen.**

PRAYERS OF INTERCESSION

The name of your son Jesus is our power.
Give this world the power to follow the Master's example;
to love as he did,
to speak as he spoke,
to behave as he behaved,
so that this world can become more
like the world you envisioned.

The name of your son Jesus is our power.
Give this world the power
to act on behalf of your Son,
to speak the truth in love,
to seek out justice when an injustice arises,
to discern your will,
and to be the living witness
of Jesus Christ.

The name of your son Jesus is our power.
Give this world the power
to honor your Son's name,
as we are one family
whose successes and achievements
reflect that we are sons and daughters of God,
brothers and sisters of Jesus,
and are the joy of the whole body.

The name of your son Jesus is our power.
Give this world the power of your name,
that name that is so powerful
it can heal the sick,
destroy all evil,
give freedom to those in chains,
and save each one of us.
The name of your son Jesus is our power.
Thank you, O God, for the name of Jesus. Amen.

INVITATION TO THE OFFERING

Today and every day,
we see signs of God's grace and abundance.
But we also know that there is suffering and need
     in the world.
Give freely of what you have been given,
as a witness to God's actions in the world.

PRAYER OF THANKSGIVING/DEDICATION

Blessed be the Lord,   *Ps. 1:3*
for God is good,
and God's love endures forever.
Our Creator, help us to mirror your goodness
through this offering, in the world. **Amen.**

CHARGE

If it had not been for the Lord who was on our side,   *Ps. 124:1;*
we would not have been freed or blessed.   *Mark 9:42–50*
Do not be a stumbling block;
be salt, have salt in yourselves,
and be at peace with one another.

BLESSING

May God, who is our strength,
help us celebrate the freedom we have received,
and remember his great deeds and grow in trust.
May Jesus Christ, in whose name we find power,
help us to honor his name with everything we do and say.
And may the Holy Spirit, who helps us to pray,
motivate in us the practice of prayer,
discovering, while praying,
that there is indeed power in the name of Jesus.

Questions for Reflection

How can you see God as an active presence in your life and in the life of
others? How can you be grateful and adore God not only in the times
when you are the subject of God's blessing but also in times of trouble and
tribulation?

Household Prayer: Morning

May the first words in my mouth today
be the sound of the name of Jesus.
Lead me to reflect on his power
as I seek to live my day,
honoring the One
who gave me salvation and a new life.
In his powerful name I pray. Amen.

Household Prayer: Evening

God, was I an agent of hope and salvation to others
as you have been to me?
As the day winds down,
help me to think about those times during the day
when I lived in your grace
and the times when I failed to be salt in your world.
Keep on working in my life,
through the power of your Holy Spirit,
so that I can become more like you want me to be.
In the name of Jesus. Amen.

Proper 21

(Sunday between September 25 and October 1 inclusive)

COMPLEMENTARY

Numbers 11:4–6, 10–16, 24–29   James 5:13–20
Psalm 19:7–14   Mark 9:38–50

OPENING WORDS / CALL TO WORSHIP

Upon this gathering of your people,   *Num. 11:16–29*
pour out your Spirit, O Lord.
Be near to us and speak to us,
and we will proclaim your glory.

CALL TO CONFESSION

In faithful prayer there is power to save the sick;   *Jas. 5:15–16*
anyone who has committed sins will be forgiven.
Therefore let us confess our sins
and pray for one another
so that we may be healed.

PRAYER OF CONFESSION

God, our strength and savior,   *Ps. 19:12–14;*
you know our great transgressions,   *Mark 9:43–47*
our hidden faults, our secret sins.
With our hands we grasp at power;
with our feet we stumble into evil;
with our eyes we look out for ourselves.
Forgive us, gracious God,
and lead us in your holy way
of life and love and peace;
for the sake of Jesus Christ our Lord. Amen.

DECLARATION OF FORGIVENESS

Though we wander from the truth,   *Jas. 5:19–20*
God brings us back

and saves our souls from death.
In the name of Jesus Christ, we are forgiven.
Thanks be to God.

PRAYER OF THE DAY

God of unquenchable fire *Mark 9:38–50*
and overflowing grace,
cast out the demons that oppress us;
take away the things that make us stumble.
Lead us into your realm of life
and season us with your peace;
in the name of Christ our Lord. **Amen.**

PRAYER FOR ILLUMINATION

Lord God, by the power of your Spirit, *Num. 11:25;*
enlighten our eyes, instruct our minds, *Ps. 19:7–8, 14*
rejoice our hearts, and revive our souls
so that our lips and our lives
may bear witness to your Word. **Amen.**

PRAYERS OF INTERCESSION

Scripture promises us *Jas. 5:13–20*
that the prayers of God's people
are powerful and effective.
In this hope, we call on God's name, saying:
Pour out your healing grace, O Lord;
send forth your Spirit to save us.

For those who are sick and suffering . . .
Pour out your healing grace, O Lord;
send forth your Spirit to save us.

For those who are burdened by sin . . .
Pour out your healing grace, O Lord;
send forth your Spirit to save us.

For nations, crumbling in conflict . . .
Pour out your healing grace, O Lord;
send forth your Spirit to save us.

For neighbors, divided by fear . . .
Pour out your healing grace, O Lord;
send forth your Spirit to save us.

For the church, longing for renewal . . .
Pour out your healing grace, O Lord;
send forth your Spirit to save us.

For the earth, groaning for peace . . .
Pour out your healing grace, O Lord;
send forth your Spirit to save us.

God of new life, raise us up
in the power of the risen Lord
so that we may lift our hearts again
in songs of thanks and praise;
through Jesus Christ our Savior. **Amen.**

INVITATION TO THE OFFERING

Through loving deeds and generous acts,   *Mark 9:38–41*
we become a blessing to others
and give honor to Christ's name.
What greater reward could we ask
than to share in God's saving work?

PRAYER OF THANKSGIVING/DEDICATION

Your gift of life, O God,   *Ps. 19:10*
is more precious than gold
and sweeter than honey to our lips.
Take these gifts of our lives:
refine and purify them,
and let them be for the world
a sign of your goodness and grace;
through Jesus Christ our Lord. **Amen.**

CHARGE

Let the name of Christ   *Mark 9:38–41*
be the word you speak,
the grace you show,
and the love you share. **Amen.**

BLESSING

Num. 11:25

May the spirit of the Lord rest upon you,
the word of the Lord live within you,
and the glory of the Lord shine around you,
this day and always. **Alleluia!**

Questions for Reflection

Numbers 11:24–29 and Mark 9:38–41 are both concerned with expressions of divine power that occur outside the bounds of formal leadership and authority. Where have you experienced God's mighty or gracious action in the church and in the world? What does it mean for the church to pray or act in the name of Jesus Christ? How do you account for gifts of the Spirit that seem to spill out beyond the church's control?

Household Prayer: Morning

God of heavenly glory,
brighter than the midday sun,
as each day tells your wonder,
may the words of my mouth
be acceptable to you,
my rock and my redeemer. Amen.

Household Prayer: Evening

God of heavenly glory,
deeper than the midnight dark,
as each night sings your mystery,
may the dreams of my heart
be acceptable to you,
my rock and my redeemer. Amen.

Proper 22

(Sunday between October 2 and October 8 inclusive)

SEMICONTINUOUS

Job 1:1; 2:1–10   Hebrews 1:1–4; 2:5–12
Psalm 26   Mark 10:2–16

OPENING WORDS / CALL TO WORSHIP
Long ago, God spoke to our ancestors through
   the prophets,   *Heb. 1:1–4; 2:5–12*
but in the last days he has spoken to us through
his Son Jesus Christ.
Jesus is the reflection of God's glory,
and he sustains all things in the world by his
   powerful Word.
It was fitting that God, for whom and through whom
   all things exist,
should give his only son to suffering for our salvation.
Therefore we will proclaim God's name.
In the midst of the congregation, we will praise God.

CALL TO CONFESSION
In God, we find light for our darkness,   *Ps. 26:2*
and through that light we discover
the things that separate us from God.
And so we ask God to prove us and try us,
and to test our hearts and minds,
that we may receive forgiveness.

PRAYER OF CONFESSION
You gave us commandments, God of love,   *Mark 10:2–16*
because you know the hardness of our hearts.
You have created us to live in community,

and still we oppress others and separate ourselves
from each other and from you.
Jesus loved the children,
but there are still children in the world
who live in hunger or fear, rejected and unloved.
Forgive us, and call us to faithfulness.
Bind all your children together as sisters and brothers,
and nurture us with your love and forgiveness,
that we might share what we have been given,
and receive your kingdom
with the wonder and gratitude of children.
In Jesus' name we pray. Amen.

DECLARATION OF FORGIVENESS

Jesus said, Let the children come to me,   *Mark 10:13–16*
do not stop them;
for it is to such as these that the kingdom of
    God belongs.
Seeing our repentant hearts,
Jesus will embrace us in grace
and comfort us with mercy.
In Jesus Christ we are forgiven.
We are children of God! Live in peace!

PRAYER OF THE DAY

God, sometimes we do not understand   *Job 1:1; 2:1–10*
why bad things happen to good people.
Sometimes all we can do
is lift up our eyes and hearts to heaven,
and scream out loud, Why?
Sometimes we do not want to persist in our integrity;
we allow our suffering to lead us into despair.
Yet wisdom comes from listening to your Word.
Enable us to see the life you have given us
through the laughter, joy, trial, and tribulation
of your son Jesus Christ,
who lived, suffered, died, and was raised for us.
In his name we pray. **Amen.**

PRAYER FOR ILLUMINATION

Long ago, God spoke to our ancestors,   *Heb. 1:1–4; 2:5–12*
but in these last days God has spoken to us
through Jesus Christ.
Open our hearts and minds to your Word,
that we may see your light. **Amen.**

PRAYERS OF INTERCESSION

We pray for those who are suffering,
through sickness, through loss,
without support, in loneliness.
Vindicate them, O Lord.

We pray for those who seek justice,
who frown upon evil
but are still shunned and persecuted.
Vindicate them, O Lord.

We pray for those who feel like the smallest of the small,
the weakest of the weak,
those who feel ignored and unloved.
Vindicate them, O Lord.

We pray for those who have been abandoned or abused,
who have been neglected and left powerless,
who have been limited or rejected.
Vindicate them, O Lord.

Take them into your arms
as Jesus did with the children,
and bless them every day
so that they are supported,
liberated,
loved,
and accepted.
In the name of the one who welcomed the children. **Amen.**

INVITATION TO THE OFFERING

In gratitude for all God has done,
and so we are invited,
we bring our offerings and tithes
for the building up of God's kingdom.

PRAYER OF THANKSGIVING/DEDICATION

Blessed are you, our Comfort.
You have given Jesus, your only son,
who was made lower than the angels,
for our sake.
With thanksgiving, we give of what you have provided,
that your will may be done in this world.
Give us the wisdom and courage to do so.
In the name of Jesus we pray. **Amen.**

CHARGE

Go out into the world   *Mark 10:2–16*
and live as children,
dependent on God and on each other,
obedient to the will of God,
holding tight to God's hand,
citizens of the kingdom.

BLESSING

May God, our Caretaker, be with us through
    good and bad,
giving us wisdom to recognize each lesson and
    each blessing.
May Jesus Christ, our Child Minder,
embrace us each day in his loving arms that make us
    feel as if we belong,
as if we are loved, as if we have a home.
May the Holy Spirit, our Counselor,
continually show us God's actions in our lives
as we are reconciled to one another,
brothers and sisters, one family, in God.

Questions for Reflection

How do we persist in our integrity when the hard times come? If we receive the good things that God provides for us, what can we do with the bad things that happen in our lives? What is God's relationship to the difficulties that we encounter?

Household Prayer: Morning

Help us, God,
as we rise this day,
to seek out your will
as we enjoy the good
and suffer through the bad.
Prove us, O God, and try us
so that we can learn the steps we need to take
to follow your ways. Amen.

Household Prayer: Evening

When I felt like a dejected child,
rejected and lost,
your comfort surrounded me,
and I felt as if I was home.
Thank you for your embracing heart,
for making me feel special and loved,
for helping me up,
and for saying that you are my brother,
my Savior, my friend.
Thank you, Jesus. Amen.

Proper 22

(Sunday between October 2 and October 8 inclusive)

COMPLEMENTARY

Genesis 2:18–24   Hebrews 1:1–4; 2:5–12
Psalm 8   Mark 10:2–16

OPENING WORDS / CALL TO WORSHIP
To my sisters and brothers   *Ps. 8:1, 9; Heb. 2:12*
I will tell your glory:
O Lord our God,
how majestic is your name!
In the great congregation
I will sing your praise:
O Lord our God,
how majestic is your name!

CALL TO CONFESSION
We have an advocate on high: Jesus Christ,   *Heb. 1:3–4, 9*
who stooped down to save us from our sin
but rose in honor and glory to reign forever.
Therefore let us seek God's grace.

PRAYER OF CONFESSION
Loving God, you created us   *Gen. 2:18–24;*
to live in relationship with you,   *Mark 10:2–12*
to love and serve one another,
and to care for all your creatures.
Yet, in the hardness of our hearts,
we dismiss your commandments
and seek to go our separate ways.
Lord, have mercy on us.
Redeem, restore, and re-create us,
for the sake of Christ our Savior. Amen.

DECLARATION OF FORGIVENESS

What are we that God is mindful of us? *Ps. 8:4; Heb. 2:6,*
Who are we that God should care for us? *10–12*
Yet God now calls us beloved children;
Jesus now claims us as sisters and brothers.
This is the good news of God's grace:
In Jesus Christ we are forgiven.
Thanks be to God.

PRAYER OF THE DAY

Faithful God, we give you thanks *Mark 10:2–16*
that nothing can separate us from your love.
Receive us as beloved children
so that we may enter your presence this day
and abide with you forever;
through Jesus Christ our Lord. **Amen.**

PRAYER FOR ILLUMINATION

Lord God, as you spoke long ago *Heb. 1:1–2*
through the voices of your prophets,
speak to us here, speak to us now,
through the power of your Spirit
and the promise of your Son,
Jesus Christ our Savior. **Amen.**

PRAYERS OF INTERCESSION

Knowing the grace of Jesus Christ, *Mark 10:14*
we entrust our lives to God, saying:
We are your children; hear our prayer.

God of creation,
protect this earth from pollution and destruction;
especially . . .
We are your children; **hear our prayer.**

God of peace,
deliver the nations from poverty and violence;
especially . . .
We are your children; **hear our prayer.**

God of redemption,
build up your church in faith and faithfulness;
especially . . .
We are your children; **hear our prayer.**

God of healing,
soothe the suffering with tenderness and strength;
especially . . .
We are your children; **hear our prayer.**

All this we ask in the name of the one
who welcomes us, as beloved children,
into the eternal glory of your realm:
 Jesus Christ our Lord. **Amen.**

INVITATION TO THE OFFERING
The heavens and the earth,   *Ps. 8*
the sun and moon and stars,
the beasts of the field,
the birds of the air,
the fish of the sea—
all things belong to God,
and to God all things return.

PRAYER OF THANKSGIVING/DEDICATION
Lord God, you have entrusted us   *Ps. 8:6*
with the works of your own hands.
Now we return these gifts to you
with thanksgiving and praise.
Use them all for your glory
and for the good of your world;
through Jesus Christ our Savior. **Amen.**

CHARGE
Come to Christ as a little child,   *Mark 10:14–15*
and you will find welcome
in the realm of God. **Amen.**

BLESSING

May the grace of God lift you up;   *Mark 10:16*
may the love of God hold you close;
may the blessing of God be yours forever. **Alleluia!**

Questions for Reflection

We were created to live in relationship—with neighbors, friends, loved ones, and above all with God. Think about the relationships in your life. Where do you find help and partnership (Gen. 2:18)? Where do you feel the strain of separation (Mark 10:9)? Who do you allow to get close to you, and who do you turn away (Mark 10:13–16)? In what ways do those relationships reflect your relationship with God?

Household Prayer: Morning

Lord Jesus, my brother,
bone of my bone,
stand with me this day,
and let me walk with you
all my life. Amen.

Household Prayer: Evening

Lord Jesus, my brother,
flesh of my flesh,
stay with me this night,
and let me rest with you
in eternal life. Amen.

Proper 23

(Sunday between October 9 and October 15 inclusive)

SEMICONTINUOUS

Job 23:1–9, 16–17	Hebrews 4:12–16
Psalm 22:1–15	Mark 10:17–31

OPENING WORDS / CALL TO WORSHIP

God, you are holy, *Ps. 22:3–5*
enthroned on the praises of Israel.
In you our ancestors trusted;
they trusted you, and you delivered them.
To you they cried, and they were saved;
in you they trusted and were not put to shame.
God, you are holy.
All praise to you, now and forever!

CALL TO CONFESSION

God is not far from us. *Ps. 22:11*
When trouble is near,
God is our help and our refuge.
Let us confess our sins to God,
that we might receive mercy.

PRAYER OF CONFESSION

We know the commandments: *Mark 10:19–22*
You shall not murder;
you shall not commit adultery;
you shall not steal;
you shall not bear false witness;
you shall not defraud;
honor your father and your mother.

We are sure we follow them,
but instead, we cannot let go

of the things we think we need
or what we think is important.
We do not follow you, or love you, O God,
with all our hearts, our minds, our strength.
We refrain from giving our whole selves to you.

Forgive our disobedience,
our lack of commitment,
and our desire to focus on material things
instead of on your will for us.
In the name of our Teacher, Jesus Christ,
who gave his whole life for the sake of the gospel. Amen.

DECLARATION OF FORGIVENESS

We do not have a high priest   *Heb. 4:15–16*
who is unable to sympathize with our weakness,
but we have one
who in every respect has been tested as we are,
yet without sin.
Therefore, you can approach the throne of grace
with boldness,
and you will receive mercy
and find grace in your time of need.
In Jesus Christ we find the forgiveness we seek.

PRAYER OF THE DAY

Listening God,   *Job 23:1–9*
hear your church today
as we bring our joys and our concerns,
our thanksgivings and our demands.
Fill us with the assurance
that you truly hear our words and thoughts,
our songs and our tears.
In the name of the one who always shows us the way,
Jesus Christ our Lord. **Amen.**

PRAYER FOR ILLUMINATION

Your word, O God, is living and active, *Heb. 4:12–13*
sharper than any two-edged sword,
piercing and able to judge the thoughts
and intentions of the heart.
May your Word be for us today
life and action,
beacon and gavel.
In the name of the Living Word we pray. **Amen.**

PRAYERS OF INTERCESSION

Have you ever felt forsaken?
Have you felt that God is far away
and cannot hear your words?
Yet the Lord hears when we call;
God answers our prayers.
Let us pray together, saying,
Hear our prayers, O Lord; answer when we call.

Have you complained to God
about the way you have been mistreated
unjustly and unfairly?
Hear our prayers, O Lord; **answer when we call.**

Have you come to God
and felt like the burden of following God's will
is too much to bear,
and have left you in shock and grieving?
Hear our prayers, O Lord; **answer when we call.**

Do not be afraid.
God's grace will find you in your time of need,
because what is impossible for us
is possible for God.
Ask with courage.
God is listening.
[A time of silence is kept.]
Thank you for hearing our prayers, O Lord,
for answering when we call. Amen.

INVITATION TO THE OFFERING

All that we have—   *Mark 10:21*
our lives, our possessions—
comes from God, to whom we owe everything.
Come, then, and give,
for Scripture tells us that in giving,
we will have treasure in heaven.
Come! Give!

PRAYER OF THANKSGIVING/DEDICATION

Gracious God,   *Mark 10:21–30*
we present these gifts and renew our commitment
to leave everything behind and follow you.
Give us the courage to fulfill your will
so that with everything we do and say
we can become a living offering
worthy of being called your disciples. **Amen.**

CHARGE

Let us hold fast to confessing   *Heb. 4:14–16*
that Jesus is the Son of God,
brought to this earth to understand our weaknesses
and to show us how to live as his disciples.
Be bold and courageous,
trusting in God's grace, love, and mercy.

BLESSING

May God bless you, providing you with a listening ear.
May Christ bless you, giving you the words you need to
    truly follow in his way.
May the Holy Spirit bless you, instilling in you the
    boldness to seek God's grace and mercy.
May the triune God bless you and give you peace.

Questions for Reflection

How do you talk to God when you feel that God is not listening? How can you be a better disciple, considering the radical words of Jesus in Mark that you have to sell all you own, give the money to the poor, and then follow him?

Household Prayer: Morning

As I open my eyes,
I want to feel your Word,
living and active and guiding my way.
I want to live knowing
that what is impossible for me is possible for you.
I want to live with the certitude
that those who are first will be last,
and the last will be first.
Give me the courage and the hope
to live with your words in my mind
for the rest of the day.
In Jesus Christ, my teacher, I pray. Amen.

Household Prayer: Evening

As I lay down to rest,
I look at the times in my day
when my heart has felt like fainting,
and I have felt like arguing,
but I do so with the understanding
that even in my deepest sorrow
you were with me.
Thank you, God, for understanding
and for helping this human being who,
if imperfectly,
strives to seek out your face,
to follow your will,
and to understand your Word.
Give me the rest I need
to live day by day
and step by step.
In the name of my example and my strength,
Jesus Christ. Amen.

Proper 23

(Sunday between October 9 and October 15 inclusive)

COMPLEMENTARY

Amos 5:6–7, 10–15   Hebrews 4:12–16
Psalm 90:12–17   Mark 10:17–31

OPENING WORDS / CALL TO WORSHIP
Seek good and not evil;   *Amos 5:6, 14–15*
seek the Lord and live!
May the Lord our God be with us.
Seek good and not evil,
that justice may prevail.
May the Lord our God show us grace.

CALL TO CONFESSION
We have a great high priest   *Heb. 4:14–16*
who can sympathize with our weakness:
Jesus, God's Son, our Savior.
Therefore, with confidence,
let us confess our sin.

PRAYER OF CONFESSION
God of justice and mercy, we confess   *Amos 5:6–7, 10–15;*
that we put ourselves first   *Mark 10:21, 31*
and trust in things that will not last.
We desire the evil and scorn the good;
we gather up power and wealth
and push aside the needy in our way.
O Lord, be gracious to us
in spite of our great sin.
Teach us to love your justice
and share in your mercy.
Help us to seek the treasure
of heavenly life with you;
through Jesus Christ our Savior. Amen.

DECLARATION OF FORGIVENESS

We have a great high priest   *Heb. 4:14*
who has passed through the heavens:
Jesus, God's Son, our Savior.
In Jesus Christ we are forgiven.
Thanks be to God.

PRAYER OF THE DAY

You alone are holy, O God;   *Mark 10:17–31*
you alone are good.
Help us to let go of worldly goods
and leave lesser things behind
so that we may be ready
to enter your holy realm
on that day when the first are last
and the last are first;
through Jesus Christ we pray. **Amen.**

PRAYER FOR ILLUMINATION

Reveal to us your Word, O God,   *Heb. 4:12*
living and active in our world
by the power of your Holy Spirit.
Let your Word pierce our hearts
and open our minds,
dividing good from evil,
truth from falsehood,
life from death;
through Jesus Christ our Lord. **Amen.**

PRAYERS OF INTERCESSION

Sometimes the troubles of the world   *Heb. 4:16;*
seem impossible to address,   *Mark 10:26–27*
and the burdens of our lives
seem too much for us to bear.
Yet we trust that, for God,
all things are possible.
God alone can save us.

Therefore we are bold to pray, saying,
God of mercy, be gracious to us.

We pray for peace among the nations,
food for the hungry,
justice for the poor,
and a life of dignity for all people.
God of mercy, **be gracious to us.**

We pray for new life in the church,
fresh energy in mission,
faithfulness in ministry,
and reconciliation in the body of Christ.
God of mercy, **be gracious to us.**

We pray for the welfare of this community,
safe streets and homes,
good schools and jobs,
and the spirit of love among neighbors.
God of mercy, **be gracious to us.**

We pray for the healing of all who suffer,
comfort for the afflicted,
hope for the despairing,
and strength for those who care for them.
God of mercy, **be gracious to us.**

O God, in whom all things are possible,
we commend these prayers to you
and commit our lives to seek your will;
through Jesus Christ our Savior. **Amen.**

INVITATION TO THE OFFERING

As followers of Jesus, we are called   *Mark 10:21*
to give ourselves for others,
as Jesus has given himself for us.
With gratitude for Christ's grace,
let us offer our lives to the Lord.

PRAYER OF THANKSGIVING/DEDICATION

God of glorious power and wisdom,   *Ps. 90:12–17*
how can we number your countless gifts?
Look upon our lives with favor,

and, by the gift of your grace,
prosper the work of our hands;
we ask this in Jesus' name. **Amen.**

CHARGE

Jesus says: Come, follow me.   *Amos 5:6; Mark 10:21*
Let us seek the Lord and live! **Amen.**

BLESSING

May God, the first and the last,   *Mark 10:31*
the beginning and the end,
the Alpha and the Omega,
be with you now and forever. **Alleluia!**

Questions for Reflection

For the prophet Amos, the city gate (Amos 5:10, 12, 15) is a place of judgment: a place to discern and decide between good and evil, justice and injustice, righteousness and sin. Jesus has similar things to say about entrance into the kingdom of God (Mark 10:23–25): a difficult choice is required—letting go of privilege, power, and possessions. What have you left behind to follow Jesus? How would you describe what Bonhoeffer calls "the cost of discipleship"?

Household Prayer: Morning

Steadfast, loving God,
in the morning I sing your praise.
Give me wisdom for this day
and rejoice in me,
as I rejoice in you. Amen.

Household Prayer: Evening

Steadfast, loving God,
in the evening I bless your name.
Give me grace for this night
and abide with me,
as I abide in you. Amen.

Proper 24

(Sunday between October 16 and October 22 inclusive)

SEMICONTINUOUS

Job 38:1–7 (34–41)   Hebrews 5:1–10
Psalm 104:1–9, 24, 35c   Mark 10:35–45

OPENING WORDS / CALL TO WORSHIP
Praise the Lord, for God is great indeed!   *Ps. 104:1–9*
Let us sing praises for God's glorious works.
We give glory, honor, and thanksgiving to the Lord,
who makes and sustains all things.

CALL TO CONFESSION
Let us confess our sins against God and our neighbor,
trusting in the mercy of our Lord.

PRAYER OF CONFESSION
Merciful and gentle God,   *Mark 10:35–37;*
we have wanted reward without sacrifice.   *Heb. 5:2*
We have been unwilling to serve and
have not humbled ourselves in obedience.
Forgive our hubris, gracious God.
Correct our ignorant ways
and help us to know your glory through servanthood.
Guide us to be true followers of your way,
through Jesus Christ our Lord. Amen.

DECLARATION OF FORGIVENESS
People of God, your sins are forgiven,   *Heb. 5:2*
for the Lord who made all things knows our
     weaknesses.
Therefore, turn away from sin and obey the ways
     of the Lord.
Be reconciled to the community in service and love.

PRAYER OF THE DAY

O God, you show us the way of servanthood. *Mark 10:43–44*
You have given us much so that we can bless others
and not seek gratification for ourselves.
Help us to seek your path and keep us in humility
so that we can be the light of Christ in the world.
In the name of the one who came to serve, we pray. **Amen.**

PRAYER FOR ILLUMINATION

O God, *Job 38:1*
your Word gives us counsel for our understanding.
Enable us to receive it today,
in the name of your son, our Lord. **Amen.**

PRAYERS OF INTERCESSION

[Silence is kept after each petition.]
Dear Lord Jesus Christ, you are our high priest *Heb. 5:7*
who offered yourself for us
with your prayers and tears, your very body.
Help us to pray and offer supplication for ourselves
and our community.

We pray for the local, national, and global church—
that it might exhibit the way of service in faith and love.

We pray for the international community—
that it might learn the way of peace.

We pray for anyone who suffers—
help us be the healing they need.

We pray for the earth—
help us to be proper stewards of your creation.

We remember those who have come to their eternal rest,
and we wrap our loving arms of comfort around those who grieve.

We lift up, in silence, any prayers we hold in the corners of our hearts—
for you know and understand all things.

We ask all these things in the name of our Creator,
our servant-priest Jesus, and the Holy Spirit. **Amen.**

INVITATION TO THE OFFERING
God is ever faithful
and has blessed us with so much.
With grateful hearts,
let us offer back to God what we have,
with love and thanksgiving.

PRAYER OF THANKSGIVING/DEDICATION
Gracious God,
we offer you these gifts.
Multiply them so that they might help build your
    kingdom on earth
and be of service to the body of Christ,
in whose name we pray. **Amen.**

CHARGE
The Son of Man came to serve, not to be served.   *Mark 10:45*
Let us follow Christ's example,
and give our all to God and one another.

BLESSING
May the knowledge and love of the one   *Job 38*
who knit the earth together
rest with you and give you strength to help others,
for the glory of God.

Questions for Reflection

What can you do to seek God's wisdom? How can you be a better servant?

Household Prayer: Morning

Gracious God,
keep me humble throughout the day.
Help me to seek your wisdom
as I stand in service to others.
In your name I pray. Amen.

Household Prayer: Evening

Loving God,
thank you for keeping me today.
Thank you for the awesome works you have blessed my eyes to see.
Continue to bless my community and me throughout the night.
In the name of Jesus I pray. Amen.

Proper 24

(Sunday between October 16 and October 22 inclusive)

COMPLEMENTARY

Isaiah 53:4–12	Hebrews 5:1–10
Psalm 91:9–16	Mark 10:35–45

OPENING WORDS / CALL TO WORSHIP

The Lord is our dwelling place,   *Ps. 91:9–16*
a home of peace and plenty.
The Lord is our dwelling place,
a refuge when trouble is near.
The Lord is our dwelling place,
a temple that will stand forever.

CALL TO CONFESSION

Like sheep we all have gone astray,   *Isa. 53:6*
but like a faithful, loving shepherd,
God seeks us out and calls us home.
Let us confess our sin.

PRAYER OF CONFESSION

Lord Jesus Christ, you know our sin.   *Mark 10:35–45*
We want you to do whatever we ask of you,
but we are unwilling to do what you ask of us.
We want to sit beside you in your glory,
but we fail to stand beside you in your suffering.
We want to be first in your great kingdom,
but we are among the last to serve the least.
Forgive us. Pour out your mercy upon us
and wash us clean in your saving grace.
All this we ask in your holy name. Amen.

DECLARATION OF FORGIVENESS

Hear the promise of the Lord: *Ps. 91:14–16*
Those who love me, I will deliver.
When you call me, I will answer.
I will rescue you from danger
and show you my salvation.
Believe this good news:
In Jesus Christ we are forgiven.
Thanks be to God.

PRAYER OF THE DAY

We give you thanks and praise, O God, *Mark 10:38–39*
that you have called us to this place
to hear the promise of your holy word,
to be immersed in the font of your grace,
and to drink the cup of your blessing.
Draw us deeper into your presence
and send us out to love and serve;
for the sake of Jesus Christ our Lord. **Amen.**

PRAYER FOR ILLUMINATION

O Lord, by the power of your Spirit, *Ps. 91:12, 16*
lift us up into your presence
to hear the promise of your word
and know the joy of your salvation;
through Jesus Christ our Lord. **Amen.**

PRAYERS OF INTERCESSION

In the days of his flesh, *Heb. 5:1–10; Ps. 91:16*
Jesus prayed, with loud cries and tears,
to the one who was able to save him from death.
Now enthroned in heaven,
Jesus hears our prayers, our cries, our tears,
offering salvation to all who trust in him.

Therefore we pray:
Satisfy us, O Lord, with your gift of life,
and show us your salvation.

With all who are persecuted and oppressed
we pray for justice, freedom, and peace. . . .
Satisfy us, O Lord, with your gift of life,
and show us your salvation.

With all who are afflicted with sickness or sorrow
we pray for healing, comfort, and hope. . . .
Satisfy us, O Lord, with your gift of life,
and show us your salvation.

With all who work for the good of the community
we pray for vision, strength, and joy. . . .
Satisfy us, O Lord, with your gift of life,
and show us your salvation.

With all who humbly serve the last and least
we pray for faithfulness, patience, and love. . . .
Satisfy us, O Lord, with your gift of life,
and show us your salvation.

All this we pray through Jesus Christ,
the source of our eternal salvation
and our great high priest forever. **Amen.**

INVITATION TO THE OFFERING
Jesus said: Those who wish to be great   *Mark 10:43–44*
must become servants to all.
With humility and hope
let us offer the gifts of our lives to the Lord.

PRAYER OF THANKSGIVING/DEDICATION
Holy God, we give you thanks   *Heb. 5:1–10*
for all your gifts of goodness and grace.
Receive these gifts from our hands
as a sacrifice of praise to you
and teach us to honor you each day
by our obedience to your will;
through Christ our Lord we pray. **Amen.**

CHARGE

Follow the Lord Jesus Christ,   *Mark 10:35–40*
giving glory to God alone. **Amen.**

BLESSING

The Lord deliver and protect you.   *Ps. 91:14–16*
The Lord answer you when you call.
The Lord satisfy you with long life
and offer you salvation. **Alleluia!**

Questions for Reflection

James and John, elsewhere called "Sons of Thunder" (see Mark 3:17), ask
to sit at Jesus' side and share in his glory (Mark 10:35–37). Jesus, in turn,
asks whether they are able to drink his cup or be baptized with his baptism
(Mark 10:38). Isaiah's song of the Suffering Servant has similar themes:
"Therefore I will allot him a portion with the great . . . because he poured
out himself to death" (Isa. 53:12). What does it mean to share in Christ's
glory? What does it mean to share in his cup or his baptism?

Household Prayer: Morning

Lord Most High, guard my way
and guide my steps this day,
that I may serve you faithfully
and trust in your salvation. Amen.

Household Prayer: Evening

Lord Most High, be my light
and shelter me this night,
that I may know your faithfulness
and rest in your salvation. Amen.

Proper 25

(Sunday between October 23 and October 29 inclusive)

SEMICONTINUOUS

Job 42:1–6,10–17   Hebrews 7:23–28
Psalm 34:1–8 (19–22)   Mark 10:46–52

OPENING WORDS / CALL TO WORSHIP
I will bless the Lord at all times,   *Ps. 34:1–3*
God's praise will continually be in my mouth.
My soul makes its boast in the Lord,
let the humble hear and be glad.
O magnify the Lord with me,
let us exalt God's name together!

CALL TO CONFESSION
Let us confess our sins to God,
who alone has the power to save
and waits in mercy to forgive.

PRAYER OF CONFESSION
Merciful God,   *Job 42:3; Ps. 34:2;*
we have not been humble.   *Mark 10:46–48*
We have discouraged others from seeking you.
We have not sought your wisdom.
Forgive us, O God,
and teach us to boast only of you.
Help us to celebrate when others seek after you.
Give us the light of your wisdom and ways,
through Christ our Lord. Amen.

DECLARATION OF FORGIVENESS
People of God,   *Ps. 34:6*
the Lord hears, forgives, and saves.
Therefore, be reconciled to one another
and walk humbly before God.

PRAYER OF THE DAY

Merciful God, *Ps. 34:4–8*

you always hear us when we cry out.

You stay close when we are in distress.

It is you in whom we seek refuge, and you deliver us
from evil.

Let praise flow from our mouths to your ears,

for we can taste and see that you are indeed good.

All glory, praise, and honor are due to you,

O God, our redeemer and our strength. **Amen.**

PRAYER FOR ILLUMINATION

Dear God, *Job 42:5*

let us not only hear of you

but see you with our own eyes

through your Word.

In Jesus' name we pray. Amen.

PRAYERS OF INTERCESSION

[Silence is kept after each petition.]

O God,

We come to you, because we know you'll hear our cry.

We come to you, because you call us near to you.

We come to you, because you deliver and save.

We come to you now with our prayers and petitions.

We pray for the local and universal church.

Give us the humility to walk in your way.

We pray for the leaders in our nation

and the nations around the world.

Give them the courage to walk in peace.

We pray for those who are in need.

Give us ears to hear their cries and be agents of your mercy.

We pray for those who have pain.

Heal, touch, and deliver them, O God.

We remember those who have died.

Help us give comfort to those who are left behind.

We lift our hidden prayers to you in silence,
for you hear even that which is unspoken.

All glory and praise is yours now and forever. **Amen.**

INVITATION TO THE OFFERING
The Lord is indeed good,
for God has blessed us richly.
Let us offer back a portion,
in gratitude and love.

PRAYER OF THANKSGIVING/DEDICATION
God, the creator of the universe,
we offer to you these gifts
for the glory of your kingdom,
in the name of God, Father and Mother,
Son, and Holy Spirit. **Amen.**

CHARGE
People of God,   *Job 42:3, 6*
go in peace and walk humbly in the world.

BLESSING
Beloved, may the healing love of Christ,
the wisdom of God,
and the strengthening power of the Spirit
be with you this day and always.

Questions for Reflection

What can you do to bring someone to Christ? How can you help someone
find his or her healing?

Household Prayer: Morning

Dear God,
help me to follow after your ways
as I go throughout my day. Amen.

Household Prayer: Evening

Gracious God, thank you for keeping me covered throughout the day.
Grant me peace and rest in your safety.
In Jesus' name I pray. Amen.

Proper 25

(Sunday between October 23 and October 29 inclusive)

COMPLEMENTARY

Jeremiah 31:7–9	Hebrews 7:23–28
Psalm 126	Mark 10:46–52

OPENING WORDS / CALL TO WORSHIP
The Lord has filled our mouths with laughter   *Ps. 126:2–3*
and our tongues with shouts of joy.
The Lord has done great things for us,
and we are glad indeed.

CALL TO CONFESSION
The God of mercy hears our cries.
Let us confess our failings and needs to each other
and to the one who commands us to come and be healed.

PRAYER OF CONFESSION
Holy God,
you know us better than we know ourselves.
You see our need when we are blind to it.
You have made us to be yours.
In your compassion,
forgive us for our lack of faith
and the harm we do to others and to your earth.
Forgive us for turning away from your will,
for ignoring the cries of our neighbors,
for failing to listen to what is most nourishing even for ourselves.
Let our faults fall from your eyes as you open ours.
Hear this and answer,
in Jesus' holy name. Amen.

DECLARATION OF FORGIVENESS

People of God, beloved of the Lord,
the one who created you and maintains your every breath
calls you to receive mercy and be forgiven.
Go in peace, in the firm assurance of pardon,
so that today and every day your path may be strong and free,
in the name of the holy Trinity, one God, now and forever.

PRAYER OF THE DAY

God of power and mercy,
you gather your people with the love of a parent for a child.
You hear our cries in the night and in the day;
you answer with healing and hope.
Gather us into your strength
and feed us with your wisdom,
in the name of the Father, Son, and Holy Spirit,
one God, Mother of us all. **Amen.**

PRAYER FOR ILLUMINATION

God of light,
let your Holy Spirit come into our darkness
and open our hearts,
that your word may show us
the blessings you intend for all creation. **Amen.**

PRAYERS OF INTERCESSION

With reverence for Earth, with concern for those in need
    and for the whole human family,
let us pray to God, saying,
God of mercy, hear our prayer.

We give you thanks, O God, for the riches of this day,
this season, and this century in history.
Show us always how to better know your gifts
and shape them into benefits for the common good.
God of mercy, **hear our prayer.**

Equip the saints in every land and in every church for ministry.
Bring blessings on people of other faiths.

Gather all creation into unity in you
for the sake of your mission in the world.
God of mercy, **hear our prayer.**

Grant wisdom to all who lead nations and hold public office,
especially our governor, senators, representatives,
and all who run for public office with courage and generosity of spirit.
Give them the humility that speaks the truth in love.
God of mercy, **hear our prayer.**

Teach your people in every land to learn about, care about,
and pray for the struggles of all humanity and Earth itself.
We pray for those in any want, especially *[nations currently in jeopardy]*,
their neighboring countries, all refugees from war,
the wounded, medical staff, mothers and fathers caring for children,
and for all those who participate in violence
or work in diplomatic circles.
Bring peace to every people.
God of mercy, **hear our prayer.**

Feed the hungry, sustain the weary, shelter the homeless,
challenge the complacent, love the brokenhearted, and heal the sick.
God of mercy, **hear our prayer.**

Give us our daily bread: what we truly need each day.
Make us satisfied with the essentials of life,
that as we live in gratitude,
your gifts may increase our awareness of the needs of others.
God of mercy, **hear our prayer.**

Hear the prayers we offer now in silence or aloud. . . .
[A time of silence is kept.]
God of mercy, **hear our prayer.**

We thank you for our ancestors whose witness and conviction
built up the body of God through the ages.
Sustain us with the bread of life that fed them,
until we join all the saints around your bountiful table
at the end of the ages.
God of mercy, **hear our prayer.**

Receive our hopes and pleadings,
for great is your faithfulness;
we pray in the name of Christ Jesus, our Lord. **Amen.**

INVITATION TO THE OFFERING
Seeing the bounty that God has made for our good use,
let us give now our tithes and offerings
for the sake of the church and the poor.

PRAYER OF THANKSGIVING/DEDICATION
Holy God, bless our offerings with healing
that comes from your work and our hands.
We give with joy and thanks for what we have,
in the name of Jesus, our great high priest. **Amen.**

CHARGE
As you go from here, walk in the way of the Lord:
with thanksgiving, with gladness, with insight.
Turn to the great high priest with all your needs,
and pray for those who have no words today.

BLESSING
May the God who hears our needs
and answers the cries of our hearts
be with you today and always,
a sure and certain strength,
throughout all the ages.

Questions for Reflection

What particular vision do you seek? What do you want to **understand?**
And when you do see and understand, how will that knowledge, **that**
insight, pull you closer to following Jesus on the way of faith **and of peace?**

Household Prayer: Morning

Holy Jesus, when I awaken each day,
I long to sing with joy for another span of hours
to spend in your company.

I long to rejoice that you have placed before me
the gifts and obstacles the day will bring.
Give me wisdom to enter into each encounter with thanksgiving,
for you hold me in your care and give me words,
in Jesus' name. Amen.

Household Prayer: Evening

Ruler of all creation, I thank you for the time of rest beginning now,
for all that I have seen, tasted, touched, heard, and smelled this day,
and for all the people and creatures whose lives
have come into my experience.
Bless them with sufficient rest and peace,
that together we may all rise in the morning
with new strength, in Jesus' name. Amen.

Proper 26

(Sunday between October 30 and November 5 inclusive)

SEMICONTINUOUS

Ruth 1:1–18	Hebrews 9:11–14
Psalm 146	Mark 12:28–34

OPENING WORDS / CALL TO WORSHIP
The Lord offered himself—   *Heb. 9:12, 14*
once and for all—
so that our conscience can be free from all things that lead to death.
Let us freely go and worship the living God!

CALL TO CONFESSION
Let us confess our sins to God,
from whom our help comes.

PRAYER OF CONFESSION
O God, you have been faithful,   *Mark 12:33*
yet we have not loved you with our whole hearts.
You showed us how to love our fellow human beings,
yet we have not loved our neighbors as ourselves.
Turn us back to you, O God,
that we may follow your commandments;
through Christ our Lord. Amen.

DECLARATION OF FORGIVENESS
Beloved,   *Mark 12:33*
the Lord is loving, merciful, and just.
Therefore, we are reconciled to God and to one another,
that we might walk in peace and love.

PRAYER OF THE DAY
Dear Lord, you are our only hope.   *Ps. 146:3, 7–9*
Teach us to put our trust in you.
God, you are our help.

Teach us the path of righteousness
and turn us from the ways of the wicked,
for we know that you love those who do justice.
We will forever praise you for the glory of your righteous reign,
now and forever. **Amen.**

PRAYER FOR ILLUMINATION

O Lord, you are our God.   *Ruth 1:16*
By the power of your Holy Spirit,
teach us through your Word to follow after you.
In Jesus' name we pray. **Amen.**

PRAYER OF INTERCESSION

[A time of silence is kept after each petition.]
Let us pray to the Lord, saying,
God, in your mercy, hear our prayer.

O God, who is righteous and just,
you watch over us all and lift up the lowly.
You provide all our needs and are always faithful.
To you, O faithful One, we lift prayers for ourselves
   and our neighbors.

We pray for the church,
that we might execute justice,
feed the hungry, and watch over those in need. . . .
God, in your mercy, **hear our prayer.**

We pray for the world and its leaders,
that they might turn to the way of righteousness
and free those who are oppressed. . . .
God, in your mercy, **hear our prayer.**

We pray for those who are bowed down, captive, or alone.
Help us to be their keepers so that they might be lifted up. . . .
God, in your mercy, **hear our prayer.**

We pray for those who suffer in body, mind, or spirit,
that they might find restoration in your healing. . . .
God, in your mercy, **hear our prayer.**

We lift up to you the silent prayers we hold in our hearts. . . .
God, in your mercy, **hear our prayer.**

Through Jesus Christ our Lord,
in the unity of the Holy Spirit,
all praise and honor are due to you, almighty God,
now and forever. **Amen.**

INVITATION TO THE OFFERING

Our God is ever faithful
and provides everything that we need.
Let us praise the Lord through our giving,
that our offerings may be acceptable to God.

PRAYER OF THANKSGIVING/DEDICATION

Dear God,   *Ps. 146:8*
we offer you these gifts
that they might build up the work of your
    kingdom.
Make us living witnesses to the way of your
    righteous reign.
For the glory of your son, Jesus Christ,
in whose name we pray. Amen.

CHARGE

Jesus gave us the greatest of the commandments: *Mark 12:33*
Go, loving God with all your being,
and love one another and the world.

BLESSING

May the Lord continue to watch over us,   *Ps. 146:8–9*
keeping us close to him and in a just path.
In the name of God our creator, the Son, and the
    Holy Spirit.

Questions for Reflection

What does it mean to love God with all your heart, mind, and soul and
to love your neighbor as yourself? What can you do to watch out for the
oppressed, the widows, the orphans, or people less fortunate?

Household Prayer: Morning

Loving God,
help me to live by your commandments
as I strive to love you and my neighbors with all I have. Amen.

Household Prayer: Evening

Gracious Lord,
thank you for watching over me throughout the day.
Help me to meditate on your ways as I rest tonight.
In Jesus' name. Amen.

Proper 26

(Sunday between October 30 and November 5 inclusive)

COMPLEMENTARY

Deuteronomy 6:1–9	Hebrews 9:11–14
Psalm 119:1–8	Mark 12:28–34

OPENING WORDS / CALL TO WORSHIP
Happy are they   *Ps. 119:1*
whose way is blameless,
who follow the teaching of the Lord.

CALL TO CONFESSION
Jesus, our great high priest,
calls us to confess our sins,
to receive forgiveness,
and to be renewed for lives of freedom and joy.

PRAYER OF CONFESSION
Holy God, giver of all good things,
we have failed to live in thanksgiving
for Earth, for our families, for neighbors,
    and for strangers,
for the air we breathe, the water we drink, and the
    soil that grows our food.
Forgive us for sins against you, your creation,
    and our neighbors,
through disobedience to your will in word and deed.
Teach us to love the way of blamelessness
and to be happy in your steadfast love,
through Jesus Christ, our Savior and Lord. Amen.

DECLARATION OF FORGIVENESS
For the sake of Jesus Christ who died and rose for us,
God forgives you all your sin.

Through the power of the Holy Trinity alive in our midst,
God's mercy turns you toward what is good and just
so that you may love God and love your neighbor. **Amen.**

PRAYER OF THE DAY

Holy and gracious God,
you come to us with words of wisdom and of promise.
Teach us to know the gifts of our great high priest,
and lead us to love what is nourishing for all life,
in Jesus' name. **Amen.**

PRAYER FOR ILLUMINATION

Through your Word, O God,
let your Holy Spirit
open our insight,
remove our ignorance,
kindle our zeal,
and bind us to you,
in Jesus' name. **Amen.**

PRAYERS OF INTERCESSION

Let us pray for all the needs of the world, saying,
God of mercy, hear our prayer.

For the church of Christ and for people of faith
who call upon God by other names,
that where there is need and division,
your Spirit will bring understanding and reconciliation.
God of mercy, **hear our prayer.**

For Earth, for minerals, bacteria, microbes,
and all that lives and breathes in every size and shape;
for the healing of all Earth's scars and toxins;
for wisdom to deal well and equitably with every landscape.
God of mercy, **hear our prayer.**

For nations, leaders, armies, town councils,
peacekeepers and peacemakers,
legislators at all levels of government;
for voters and for people who work toward democracy;

for those who fight against change
and those who fight for changes in the name of justice.
God of mercy, **hear our prayer.**

For children and for those who are raising up children
in this complicated world,
that in the midst of their common struggles
there will be times of great joy and happiness.
God of mercy, **hear our prayer.**

For all who daily show us how to live well
and in accord with your commands.
God of mercy, **hear our prayer.**

For all who suffer in our land from hunger,
homelessness, poverty, and illness,
especially those we name before you . . . *[silence].*
God of mercy, **hear our prayer.**

For all else we hold in our hearts this day,
spoken aloud or in silence . . . *[silence].*
God of mercy, **hear our prayer.**

In thanksgiving for those who have taught us faith,
we ask you to hear our pleas and our words of gratitude.
Keep us in your care and bring us to the feast that has no end,
through Jesus Christ, who lives and reigns with you and the Holy Spirit,
now and forever. **Amen.**

INVITATION TO THE OFFERING
As Christ has given himself for us,
let us, in turn, give of ourselves for the sake of others.

PRAYER OF THANKSGIVING/DEDICATION
Bless these gifts, O Lord,
from your unfailing care for your people.
Let them be a sign of our gladness for all that we have
and all that we may offer to others,
in Jesus' name. **Amen.**

CHARGE

Love the Lord your God with all your heart,   *Deut. 6:5*
and with all your soul,
and with all your might.
Bind to yourselves,
as close as to your own bodies,
God's command to love your neighbor as yourself.

BLESSING

You are children of the great high priest,
never alone, never forgotten.

Question for Reflection

We serve a living God. This week, look each day for the presence of God
alive in the midst of God's people and the creation God has made. Where is
God at work, bringing people together for good?

Household Prayer: Morning

Holy God, on this new day,
I give you thanks for all that lies before me and those I love.
Guide us and keep us on the path that you intend.
Help us to see the journey you set before us
when the way grows dim. Amen.

Household Prayer: Evening

Gracious giver of all good things,
for all that has transpired in your world today,
I pray for peace and quiet to come where it is most needed.
I thank you for the work I have had to do
and pray for those who have no work.
I ask your presence now for rest and renewal,
in safety and calm,
that tomorrow I may again see your face in those I meet,
in Jesus' name. Amen.

All Saints

Wisdom of Solomon 3:1–9   Revelation 21:1–6a
or Isaiah 25:6–9   John 11:32–44
Psalm 24

OPENING WORDS / CALL TO WORSHIP

Fling wide the temple gates!   *Ps. 24:7–10; Isa. 25:9*
Open up the ancient doors!
The mighty and glorious one is coming.
Who is this mighty and glorious one?
This is the Lord for whom we have waited.
Let us be glad and rejoice in God.

CALL TO CONFESSION

God has promised to make of us a new creation,   *Rev. 21:1*
laying to rest the former things, making all things new.
Trusting in God's grace, let us confess our sin.

PRAYER OF CONFESSION

Almighty Lord and God, in Jesus Christ   *Isa. 25:7–9; John 11:44;*
you came from heaven to dwell among us,   *Rev. 21:2–4*
calling us to be your faithful people.
Yet we remain shrouded in sin—
we hurt and disgrace ourselves;
we abuse and destroy one another;
we dishonor your holy name.
Forgive us; unbind us and let us go
so that we may stand among your saints,
rejoicing in your saving grace;
through Jesus Christ our redeemer. Amen.

DECLARATION OF FORGIVENESS

Listen! The one who is seated on the throne says: *Rev. 21:5–6*
See, I am making all things new.
And now it is finished! Hear the good news:
In Jesus Christ we are forgiven.
Thanks be to God.

PRAYER OF THE DAY

God of all glory, we gather here today   *John 11:32–44*
with the saints of every time and place
to honor and praise your holy name.
As you have revealed your mercy and might
to your faithful people in every age,
so let us glimpse—even through our tears—
the mystery of your life-giving grace
and the love that even death cannot destroy;
through Jesus Christ, Alpha and Omega. **Amen.**

PRAYER FOR ILLUMINATION

Almighty God, your word is life   *Rev. 21:5–6a*
and your promise is trustworthy and true.
By the power of your Holy Spirit
write your word upon our hearts
so that we may be your new creation;
through Jesus Christ our Lord. **Amen.**

PRAYERS OF INTERCESSION

Watching for a new heaven,   *Isa. 25:8; Rev. 21:4*
waiting for a new earth,
we pray to the Lord, saying,
O Lord our God, have mercy,
and wipe away our tears.

We pray for the church.
Transform this broken body
into a communion of saints,
a company of the faithful,
working for good in your world.
O Lord our God, have mercy,
and wipe away our tears.

We pray for the world.
Destroy the shroud of death
that is spread over the nations.
Replace the rule of wealth and war
with your realm of justice and peace.
O Lord our God, have mercy,
and wipe away our tears.

We pray for this community.
Make your home among us;
dwell with us in this place.
Let it be a city of heavenly peace,
a place of refuge for all.
O Lord our God, have mercy,
and wipe away our tears.

We pray for loved ones.
Soothe those who are suffering;
comfort those who mourn.
Let us be glad and rejoice
in the gift of your salvation.
O Lord our God, have mercy,
and wipe away our tears.

As you have sustained your saints
through centuries of service,
keep us faithful, here and now,
until your will is done
on earth as it is in heaven;
in Jesus' name we pray. **Amen.**

INVITATION TO THE OFFERING

Who will enter the presence of the Lord?   *Ps. 24:3–5*
Who will stand in this holy place?
Those who offer their whole lives to God—
heart and mind and soul and strength—
they will receive the blessing of the Lord.

PRAYER OF THANKSGIVING/DEDICATION

The earth belongs to you, O God,   *Ps. 24:1, 5–6, 10*
the world and all its people.
For the blessings of this life
and the gift of your salvation
we give you thanks and praise.
As you have sought us out to save us
help us to seek your face among our neighbors
so that all may know the wonder of your love;
through Jesus Christ our Lord. **Amen.**

CHARGE

With a loud voice, Jesus said: Lazarus, come out!   *John 11:43*
So he calls us now: to go forth in faith and love,
living each day as a gift of God's grace,
proclaiming the gospel in word and deed. **Amen.**

BLESSING

May the Lord our God—   *Rev. 21:6*
the Alpha and Omega,
the first and the last,
the beginning and the end—
be with you this day
and forevermore. **Alleluia!**

Questions for Reflection

Tears flow through the readings for All Saints' Day in Year B of the Revised
Common Lectionary: an Old Testament prophet envisions the day when
"the Lord GOD will wipe away the tears from all faces" (Isa. 25:8); a New
Testament visionary promises the faithful that God "will wipe every
tear from their eyes" (Rev. 21:4); even Jesus weeps at the tomb of his
friend Lazarus (John 11:35). What do saints have to do with tears? Does
faithfulness demand suffering? Does it require a certain sort of compassion
for the pain of the world?

Household Prayer: Morning

As I live this day, O Lord,
let me be a sign of your salvation—
food for those who hunger,
a comfort to those who mourn.
This I ask in the name of Jesus,
the Alpha and Omega. Amen.

Household Prayer: Evening

As I rest this night, O Lord,
let me be a temple of your peace—
a home for your holy presence,
a sanctuary of renewal.
This I ask in the name of Jesus,
the Alpha and Omega. Amen.

Proper 27

(Sunday between November 6 and November 12 inclusive)

SEMICONTINUOUS

Ruth 3:1–5; 4:13–17   Hebrews 9:24–28
Psalm 127   Mark 12:38–44

OPENING WORDS / CALL TO WORSHIP

Praise the Lord! The Lord will never leave us alone.   *Ruth 4:14*
Let the name of the Lord be renowned throughout
    the earth,
now and forever.

CALL TO CONFESSION

Let us confess our sins
to the one who sacrificed for us
and waits in mercy to forgive.

PRAYER OF CONFESSION

Dear God, you gave us your only son,   *Mark 12:38–44*
yet we fail to give you our best.
You answer our prayers,
even though we pray with a haughty spirit.
You continue to bless us,
even as we ignore those in need.
Forgive us, we pray, and turn us toward you,
for the sake of Jesus Christ our Lord. Amen.

DECLARATION OF FORGIVENESS

Christ, who is our high priest,   *Heb. 9:27–28*
made himself a sacrifice once and for all for the
    forgiveness of sins.
Therefore, be reconciled to God, sin no more,
and do all things for the glory of God.

PRAYER OF THE DAY

Gracious Lord, *Ps. 127:1–2*
our labors are in vain unless you labor with us,
   O God.
Continue to bless the work of our hands,
that we might labor for the glory of your name alone,
through your son Jesus Christ, in whose name
   we pray. **Amen.**

PRAYER FOR ILLUMINATION

O God,
wash and anoint us with your word of truth.
In the name of Jesus we pray. **Amen.**

PRAYER OF INTERCESSION

[A time of silence is kept after each petition.]
Loving God,
you never leave us alone, *Ruth 4:14*
nor fail to watch out for our well-being,
restoring us and providing for us.
Because you are faithful, we come to you now
to make our petitions known to you.

We pray for the church and its leaders;
may we continue to be living witnesses for you.

We pray for the global community;
enable us to serve those in need and work for peace.

We pray for all those who are cheated and abused;
help us be advocates for the powerless, that we might
   enact godly justice.

We pray for those who suffer;
make us agents of your restoration and healing.

We pray for your creation;
make us good stewards, that many generations will know
the goodness of your gifts.

We remember those who have come to their eternal rest;
help us to comfort those who grieve their loss.

We lift up to you the prayers we hold secretly,
for we know that you know all things.

All these things we ask in Jesus' name. **Amen.**

INVITATION TO THE OFFERING
The Lord has blessed us richly.
Let us give cheerfully what we have
for the upkeep and uplift of God's kingdom.

PRAYER OF THANKSGIVING/DEDICATION
Almighty God,   *Mark 12:44*
whether we have given from abundance
or from little,
we humbly offer these gifts to you,
and for the glory of your name,
through your son Jesus Christ with the
    Holy Spirit. **Amen.**

CHARGE
Trust in the Lord   *Ps. 127:1–2*
and know that God is at work within you.

BLESSING
May the Lord continue to be a restorer of life,   *Ruth 4:15*
and watch over you
as we witness to God's blessings.

Questions for Reflection

What has God restored for you? Do you have enough faith to give when
you have a little?

Household Prayer: Morning

Dear God,
bless the labors of my hands today
so that you might get the glory. Amen.

Household Prayer: Evening

Gracious God,
thank you for blessing me throughout the day.
Please grant me a restful sleep, as I put my trust in you. Amen.

Proper 27

(Sunday between November 6 and November 12 inclusive)

COMPLEMENTARY

1 Kings 17:8–16	Hebrews 9:24–28
Psalm 146	Mark 12:38–44

OPENING WORDS / CALL TO WORSHIP

Praise the Lord! Praise the Lord, O my soul!   *Ps. 146:1–2, 5–10*
I will praise the Lord as long as I live;
I will sing praises to my God all my life long.
Happy are those whose help is the God of Jacob,
who made heaven and earth, the sea, and all that is
    in them and
who executes justice for the oppressed and
    gives food to the hungry.
The Lord sets prisoners free and lifts up those
    who are bowed down.
The Lord watches over the stranger and
    upholds the orphan and the widow.
The Lord will reign forever. Praise the Lord!

CALL TO CONFESSION

Christ came into the world to save us from sin,   *Heb. 9:26*
once and for all.
Because of his sacrifice for us,
God waits in mercy to forgive.
Let us confess our sin before God and one another.

PRAYER OF CONFESSION

Forgive us, Lord, when we think too highly
    of ourselves   *Mark 12:38–44*
and clamor after privilege and honor.
Forgive us, Lord, when we cannot lift our gaze
because we do not believe we have anything to give.

You have given us the best gift of all:
freedom from all that harms us
and the way to abundant life.
Have mercy on our foolishness
and heal our lovesick hearts,
that we may live faithfully for you.
In Jesus' name we pray. Amen.

DECLARATION OF FORGIVENESS
[Water is poured into the font.]
Sisters and brothers,
the news is good and it is for you:
in Jesus Christ,
all our failings are washed away;
our thirst for goodness is quenched.
Remember your baptism and be glad!

PRAYER OF THE DAY
All praise to you, most holy and gracious God!   *1 Kgs. 17:13–16*
You have set us free from fear
and filled us with good things.
You surprise us with your grace
and give us all we need.
Even when we lose sight of your ways,   *Mark 12:40, 44*
you pull us back to you
and overwhelm us all over again,
reminding us of your power, your compassion,
and your justice.
All praise to you, our triune God,
now and forever. **Amen.**

PRAYER FOR ILLUMINATION
By the power of your Holy Spirit
startle us with your Word, O God,
and awaken us to your truth,
for Jesus' sake. **Amen.**

PRAYERS OF INTERCESSION
Let us pray to the God who knows our needs
even before we ask, saying,
Heal us, O God; make us whole.

Our cities and nations are governed by greed;   *Mark 12:38–40*
our towns are fueled by gossip, not grace.
Heal us, O God; **make us whole.**

Our churches seek out those who are like-minded;
we allow disagreements to divide us.
Heal us, O God; **make us whole.**

Your people have become accustomed to war
and tolerant of violence in our streets and our homes.
Heal us, O God; **make us whole.**

Your children are hungry and cannot find shelter,
while their brothers and sisters seek after luxury.
Heal us, O God; **make us whole.**

We lie to ourselves and to one another.
Heal us, O God; **make us whole.**

We are felled by disease and suffer anxieties.
Heal us, O God; **make us whole.**

We are grieved by death even while we wait in hope for you.
Heal us, O God; **make us whole.**

You are trustworthy, O God, and in you is life.
For hearing our prayers, calming our fears,
and bringing us ever nearer to your realm
of peace and justice for all,
we give all thanks and praise,
now and forever. **Amen.**

INVITATION TO THE OFFERING
Freely we have received; freely we give.
With joyful hearts, let us bring our tithes and offerings to God.

PRAYER OF THANKSGIVING/DEDICATION
O God, you give us life; you are the source of every blessing.
These offerings are but a token of our gratitude to you.

Use them, and us, to work your will in this world you love,
and let all we say and do be to your glory.
In Jesus' name we pray. **Amen.**

CHARGE

Go out into the world with courage, *1 Kgs. 17:16;*
trusting God to supply your every need. *Mark 12:44*

BLESSING

May the abundant goodness of God,
the generous mercy of Christ,
and the sustaining power of the Spirit
be with you today and every day
until the coming of God's joyous reign.

Question for Reflection

Where in your life do you doubt God's power to provide what you need?

Household Prayer: Morning

With the rising sun I sing my praise to you,
O God, who gives me breath.
Keep me mindful of the ways you are at work in the world,
and use me for your purposes,
for the sake of Jesus Christ. Amen.

Household Prayer: Evening

Blessed are you, O God.
You guide the stars on their courses,
yet still you remember me.
Thank you for bringing me through this day,
and for welcoming me into this night. Amen.

Proper 28

(Sunday between November 13 and November 19 inclusive)

SEMICONTINUOUS

1 Samuel 1:4–20   Hebrews 10:11–14
1 Samuel 2:1–10   (15–18), 19–25
                         Mark 13:1–8

OPENING WORDS / CALL TO WORSHIP

Let our hearts exult in the Lord;   *1 Sam. 2:1–2*
our strength is exalted in God.
Let our mouths be ever fixed in praise;
God has given us the victory.
There is no Holy One like the Lord;
there is no Rock like our God.
Praise the Lord!

CALL TO CONFESSION

Trusting in the grace of God,
let us confess our sins against God and our neighbors.

PRAYER OF CONFESSION

O God, who is faithful and just,   *1 Sam. 2:3, 6*
we have failed to help those who have little
while we have much.
We are boastful and haughty,
and fail to appreciate the gifts you have given.
Our arrogance has led us away from your righteous way.
Forgive us, Merciful God,
and lead us to a humble path, for Jesus' sake. Amen.

DECLARATION OF FORGIVENESS

People of God,   *Heb. 10:17–19, 23*
Jesus Christ, who gave himself once and for all,
forgives and saves.

Therefore, be reconciled to one another,
holding fast to the confession of our hope,
through Christ our Lord.

PRAYER OF THE DAY

Merciful God,   *1 Sam. 1:11–15*
you hear our cries and honor our tears.
Stir in us such a passion during worship
that we might vow to give you our best,
for the glory of your name. **Amen.**

PRAYER FOR ILLUMINATION

Almighty God,   *1 Sam. 2:9*
speak your Word to us,
and guide our feet,
that we might be hearers and doers of your word. **Amen.**

PRAYERS OF INTERCESSION

[Silence is kept after each petition.]
God, in your mercy
you hear our cries
and know the hidden desires of our hearts.
You answer prayer.
We come to you, gracious Lord,
praying for ourselves and our community.

We pray for the witness of the church,
that we might live the gospel.

We pray for the global community,
that we might learn from each other and live in peace.

We pray for the needs in our local community
[insert local concerns here]
for we know that you, O God, are our provider.

We pray for those who suffer in mind, body, or spirit;
make us agents of your healing power.

We remember those who have died;
help us to comfort those who grieve.

We lift up to you the silent prayers we hold in our hearts and minds.

We ask all these things for the glory and honor of your name,
through Jesus Christ our Lord, by the power of the Holy Spirit. **Amen.**

INVITATION TO THE OFFERING
People of God,
the Lord has given us so much.
Let us praise the Lord through our gifts
for the uplift of God's kingdom.

PRAYER OF THANKSGIVING/DEDICATION
Dear God,
we offer these gifts back to you.
Multiply them so that they might help
build up your kingdom on earth.
All glory, praise, and honor are due to you,
now and forever. **Amen.**

CHARGE
Beloved,   *Heb. 10:24;*
be encouraged in the Lord,   *Mark 13:5*
and do not be led astray.
Stand firm in the witness of the gospel
and do good deeds,
all for the glory of God.

BLESSING
May the Lord continue to bless and keep you,
this day and forevermore.

Questions for Reflection

What can you do to encourage another person? What can you do to make
your prayers and worship more passionate?

Household Prayer: Morning

Dear God,
empower me to encourage others for the glory of your name
as I go throughout my day.
In Jesus' name I ask it. Amen.

Household Prayer: Evening

Dear God,
thank you for keeping me throughout the day.
Grant me a night of peaceful rest,
and put a song of praise in my heart when I wake in the morning.
In Jesus' name I pray. Amen.

Proper 28

(Sunday between November 13 and November 19 inclusive)

COMPLEMENTARY

Daniel 12:1–3	Hebrews 10:11–14
Psalm 16	(15–18), 19–25
	Mark 13:1–8

OPENING WORDS / CALL TO WORSHIP

Bless the Lord who counsels and guides us. *Ps. 16:7–11*
Because we keep the Lord ever before us,
we shall not be moved.
Rejoice! Let your hearts be glad!
Let your spirits rejoice and your bodies rest secure.
For God does not give us up to death, but shows us
the path of life.
Praise the Lord!

CALL TO CONFESSION

Since we have a great high priest, Jesus Christ, *Heb. 10:21–23*
let us approach the throne of grace in
full assurance of faith,
for God has promised to be merciful.

PRAYER OF CONFESSION

God of grace,
all around us are wars, and rumors of wars, *Mark 13:5–8*
and we are afraid for ourselves and our world.
We follow after false leaders
and grasp for whatever security we can find.
Forgive us, Lord, for we are quick to forget
that all of life is in your hands.
Renew our hope, increase our courage,
and keep us watchful for the signs
of your just and peaceful reign that is to come;
through Jesus Christ our Lord. Amen.

DECLARATION OF FORGIVENESS

Hear the good news!

[Water is poured into the font.]

Our guilty hearts have been sprinkled clean,   *Heb. 10:22*

our bodies washed with pure water.

Live in peace, forgiven and freed.

PRAYER OF THE DAY

Holy God,

creator of all that is and is to come,

you made the world and called it good.

We thank you and praise you,

for we have wreaked havoc on your good creation,

yet you promise to make all things whole   *Rev. 21:3*

and live among us in joy and peace.

Keep us watchful for Christ's coming,

enliven our hope,

and support us through the birth pangs   *Mark 13:8*

of your new creation,

that we may welcome you with songs of praise. **Amen.**

PRAYER FOR ILLUMINATION

O Lord, you have the words of eternal life.   *John 6:68*

Speak to us by the power of your Holy Spirit,

that we might hear what you would say to us today. **Amen.**

PRAYERS OF INTERCESSION

[A time of silence is kept after each petition.]

Let us join our hearts and minds in prayer, saying,

Lord, in your mercy, hear our prayer.

Source of all wisdom,

the nations are fraught with anxiety and fear,

and violence is all around us.

Guide all peoples in the way of peace. . . .

Lord, in your mercy, **hear our prayer.**

God of the covenant,

our churches are torn by disputes and mistrust.

Soothe our angry spirits and reconcile us to your will. . . .

Lord, in your mercy, **hear our prayer.**

Creator of the cosmos,
we are killing your creation with our toxic ways.
Restore your good Earth and make us better stewards
    of all you have given us. . . .
Lord, in your mercy, **hear our prayer.**

Fount of compassion,
your children suffer from diseases and addictions.
Heal us, we pray, and make us whole. . . .
Lord, in your mercy, **hear our prayer.**

Source of all life,
in spite of your promises, we fear death
and cannot help but grieve for those we have lost.
Comfort us, and restore our hope. . . .
Lord, in your mercy, **hear our prayer.**

Holy God,
you know our needs even before we ask.
Hear now our secret prayers. . . .
Lord, in your mercy, **hear our prayer.**

Keep us, O Lord, in the sure and certain hope
of your providential care
and guide us in your ways of justice, peace, and love,
until that day when we welcome Jesus Christ,
in whose name we pray. **Amen.**

INVITATION TO THE OFFERING

With glad and generous hearts,
let us bring our offerings to God.

PRAYER OF THANKSGIVING/DEDICATION

How can we thank you, O God, for all that you have done?
You give us life; you give us hope; you give us your very self.
Take our offerings—and our very selves—that your will may be done
in our church, in our community, and throughout your
wide and beautiful world.
In Jesus' name we pray. **Amen.**

CHARGE

Hold fast to hope, for God is faithful.   *Heb. 10:23–25*
Provoke one another to love and good deeds
while you wait and watch for the coming of
    Christ's reign.

BLESSING

May the blessing of God,
Father, Son, and Holy Spirit,
one God, Mother of us all,
be with you this day and forevermore.

Question for Reflection

How do you profess your faith in God's coming reign of justice and peace,
even in the face of our troubled world?

Household Prayer: Morning

Loving God,
thank you for waking me up this morning
and giving me another day to love and serve you well.
Thank you for the ways you will lead me today;
help me to trust in you. Amen.

Household Prayer: Evening

Gracious God,
you were good to me today,
even when I lost sight of you.
Forgive my fickle and heartless ways,
and conform my will to yours.
Grant me a safe rest
and strengthen me in body, mind, and heart,
that I may serve you faithfully
and love you well
when I awake to greet your new day. Amen.

Reign of Christ / Proper 29

SEMICONTINUOUS

2 Samuel 23:1–7	Revelation 1:4b–8
Psalm 132:1–12 (13–18)	John 18:33–37

OPENING WORDS / CALL TO WORSHIP

Grace to you and peace from the one who is   *Rev. 1:4b, 5*
and who was and who is to come,
and from Jesus Christ, the faithful witness,
the firstborn of the dead, and the ruler of the
    kings of the earth.
Holy, holy, holy is the Lord of hosts.   *Isa. 6:3*
The whole earth is full of God's glory.

CALL TO CONFESSION

Trusting in the power of God not only to
    fashion the world
but to mend and refashion our hearts, let us say
    how it is with us.

PRAYER OF CONFESSION

Holy One,   *John 18:33–37*
we dare to call you Lord,
but yield to you only fragments of our lives.
You had nowhere to lay your head;
we surround ourselves with comfort.
We expect to serve you with what remains
after we have indulged our desires.
Forgive our greed, our lack of trust,
our desire to pick the times and places we will
    respond to our call.
In your abundant mercy teach us what it
    means to follow,
even at the cost of our lives. Amen.

DECLARATION OF FORGIVENESS

[Water is poured into the font.]

Beloved of God, the mercy of the Lord is from
    everlasting to everlasting—
it cannot be contained, but must be poured out.
Believe this good news: in Jesus Christ, our sin
    is forgiven.
Live as a people set free.

PRAYER OF THE DAY

Sovereign God,
come to us now in silent, holy power.
Still our distracted minds, our bruised hearts,
    our longing bodies.
Then speak the power of Jesus' name
in such a way that we might hear it,
in such a way that we might bear it into the world—
as a people who seek not to preserve what we know
but to make palpable who you are—
for we move and pray by the gift of your breath
    within us. **Amen.**

PRAYER FOR ILLUMINATION

Spirit of truth,   *John 18:33–37*
move now in ancient words and cluttered hearts
that we might hear your voice and live,
for we long to be glad servants
of your hidden, holy reign.
We pray in the name of Jesus, the Prince of Peace. **Amen.**

PRAYERS OF INTERCESSION

Holy God,
we do not know how to pray,
    but Jesus invites us into the life he shares with you,
and so we keep coming, because we want to live.
Receive us now in our frailty, our complacency, our desire.

We pray for your church all over the world.
May the life we discover in you
bind us to each other and to the world you love,

for no need is beyond the strength of your call
and no child of yours is expendable.
Merciful God, give us wisdom and courage beyond our imagining.

We pray for each leader who might be an instrument of peace
in a troubled land.
By the movement of your reconciling spirit,
bless your people with the courage to reach past
old wounds and persistent fears.
God of resurrection, bring life where hope has died.

We pray for friends and strangers in the grip of addiction.
Make us able companions for each other,
and bless us with hope that bears fruit.

We pray for unsettled economies
and those whose needs are overlooked in the choices of the powerful.
May we, who know so much privilege,
bear our responsibilities with open eyes and open hands.

We pray for all who stand at the thresholds of life:
your children who are soon to be born,
and your children who are soon to go home.

We give thanks for new faces to love, ideas to ponder, work to do—
and we marvel at the sturdy friendships and persistent memories
that sustain us when the way is hard.
May each be a reminder of your love and your provision.

We thank you for the gift of song—
for notes that speak when words fail,
and choirs that practice at the end of long days.
Give strength to leaders who call forth the best from us
and invite us to breathe together.

Holy One, keep calling us into the world—your world—
as salt and light.
Equip each of us for the challenges we will face
until we learn to worship in the most unlikely places,
for you are the source of our song and the well from which we pray,
wherever we are planted.

By the power of your Spirit, we make our prayer with resurrection hope,
in the name of Jesus. **Amen.**

INVITATION TO THE OFFERING

Sisters and brothers, *Rev. 1:8*
we worship the One who stands
at the *beginning* and at the *end* of history—
the God for whom all time is *now*.
Every day we have a chance to participate
in the work God is doing in the world.
By bringing our gifts each week,
by offering our lives each day,
we affirm our trust in a power beyond violence,
beyond greed.
Let us gladly offer who we are—
and what we hold—
in service to God.

PRAYER OF THANKSGIVING/DEDICATION

Holy God, *Ps. 132:15*
the psalmist declares that in your realm,
all the poor are satisfied with bread.
Plant that promise firmly in our hearts,
that we might be agents of your covenant love.
Use these gifts, shape our desire, until hunger is no more—
for Jesus taught us to seek our neighbor's daily bread,
and we pray by the power of his name. **Amen.**

CHARGE

Sisters and brothers, *Phil. 2:5–7*
there is no greater joy in life, no greater freedom,
than to offer our lives in service to God.
Let the same mind be in us that was in Christ Jesus,
who, though he was in the form of God,
did not regard equality with God as something to be exploited,
but emptied himself, taking the form of a servant.

BLESSING

May the Lord God who is, *Rev. 1:8; 2 Sam. 23:1;*
and who was, *Ps. 132:9*

and who is to come,
the Almighty,
be your strength, your hope, and your joy,
this day and forevermore.

Questions for Reflection

Jesus said that his kingdom is not of this world and that belonging to
his way of life means a constant attentiveness to his voice. How are you
(individually and as a community) embodying the countercultural reign of
God? What is a further step that you are being called to take? How might
you make more time to listen for his voice?

Household Prayer: Morning

Gracious God,
help me to receive this day as gift:
in the tasks for which I do not feel prepared,
in the needs I am not strong enough to meet.
In my caution and in my confidence
teach me to listen for your voice and to watch for your provision.
Grant me the gift of life in community,
    that I might witness your desire flowing through others,
    that I might be joined to greater service,
for I pray in the name of Jesus, whose every breath was praise. Amen.

Household Prayer: Evening

Lord of life,
as I recollect this day,
help me to recognize your witness
in truth that challenged convenience,
in decisions that stretched my heart,
in forgiveness freely offered.
Teach me to trust the sound of your voice
and to follow where you lead,
for I would serve in the shelter of your reign. Amen.

Reign of Christ / Proper 29

COMPLEMENTARY

Daniel 7:9–10, 13–14   Revelation 1:4b–8
Psalm 93   John 18:33–37

OPENING WORDS / CALL TO WORSHIP
God established the world from of old.   *Dan. 7:14; Ps. 93:1, 2;*
God's reign shall never end.   *Rev. 1:5, 6*
God delivered us in freedom and truth.
God's love is everlasting.

CALL TO CONFESSION
Jesus loves us and frees us from our sins;   *Rev. 1:5*
therefore, let us confess our sins to God.

PRAYER OF CONFESSION
Holy God,
how often we trust in the promises of earthly rulers
instead of the power of your love;
help us to turn our hearts toward you.
Restore us in your love, and set us free
to forgive as we have been forgiven,
by the grace and mercy of Christ. Amen.

DECLARATION OF FORGIVENESS
Sisters and brothers, God loves us, forgives us,   *Rev. 1:5b*
and frees us from our sins;
therefore be at peace.

PRAYER OF THE DAY
Eternal God, Jesus taught that true power is
    made known in service:
we are to love you, our neighbors, and ourselves
as we reveal your reign of peace.

Give us the will to do this work
and the grace that we may accomplish it;
with you, in Christ, and through the Holy Spirit,
on earth as it is in heaven. **Amen.**

PRAYER FOR ILLUMINATION

Come, Holy Spirit; open our hearts to receive a
    word of truth,
then set us free to follow in the power of
    Christ's love. **Amen.**

PRAYERS OF INTERCESSION

Almighty God, you have exalted Jesus over all creation
to lead us into truth.
Receive the prayers we offer in his name
and for the world you so dearly love.

Give wisdom to all leaders and people
to resist the earthly powers that destroy our common life;
guide us in the way of peace.

Bring unity of mission to your church
and fill us with a joy for your gospel
as we invite others into your reign.

Enfold all who suffer in body, mind, or soul
into the comfort of your healing,
and enable us to extend our arms in kindness as
    witness to your love.

Eternal God, our beginning and our end,
we remember those who are dying and have died;
may they know the joy of your never-ending realm of peace.

Sovereign God, you sent Jesus
to inaugurate a world of justice and peace
through the power of your Spirit.
May the words we pray be more than words this day;
let our lives reveal your love. **Amen.**

INVITATION TO THE OFFERING

Jesus said, Everyone who belongs to the truth
   listens to my voice.   *John 18:37*
Heeding his word with grateful hearts,
let us bring our offerings to God.

PRAYER OF THANKSGIVING/DEDICATION

Holy God, you call us from every tribe,
language, people, and nation
to share in your everlasting kingdom.
Bless these gifts that we offer
that we may extend your blessing to others,
in Christ's name we pray. Amen.

CHARGE

God has made us to be a kingdom of priests
to love God and serve the world.
Go in peace to love and serve.

BLESSING

May the blessing of God,
the One who creates, redeems, and restores,
be with you now and always.

Questions for Reflection

Jesus is exalted over the whole of creation through his loving allegiance to God alone. His life, death, and resurrection reveal that true power is found through loving service, and it is this that makes him King. If his life and death give a radically new meaning to the words "king" and "kingship" and how justice is enacted in love, how does this change your understanding of power? How does it change the way you live?

Household Prayer: Morning

Loving God, it is a new day.
Awaken my desire to delight in you
by more faithfully serving your world.
Keep me alert to the earthly powers and privileges
at play in this world
as I seek to foster justice and serve your reign. Amen.

Household Prayer: Evening

Brother Jesus, I have done my best
to love and serve your realm this day.
Where I have succeeded, I give you thanks.
Where I have failed, I ask your guidance and forgiveness.
I release all my cares and fears to you this night
as you watch over your wondrous and wounded world. Amen.

❦ ADDITIONAL RESOURCES ❦

Thanksgiving for Baptism

Praise to you, O God, for the gift of water . . .
for creating this blue orb and giving it to us as a home,
for saving us from the flood and blessing us with a new start,
for leading us through the sea from slavery to freedom.

Thank you for baptizing Jesus in the waters of the Jordan,
that we might be baptized with him,
and for welcoming us to the river of the water of life,
when we will be raised with him.

By the power of your Holy Spirit,
keep us faithful until that day,
renewing us with your life-giving waters
until we enter your eternal realm,
singing songs of praise. **Amen.**

Great Prayers of Thanksgiving / Eucharistic Prayers

[These prayers are offered as supplementary resources that are intended to be in line with approved and published denominational worship materials. They may be adapted for your congregational context.]

GENERAL USE

INVITATION TO THE TABLE

Jesus calls all people to sit at table with him:
the sick and the uncertain,
the weak and the poor,
the Pharisees and tax collectors.
From north and south and east and west he calls us
to come and sit at this table,
the foretaste of the kingdom of God.

On a night long ago, when Jesus sat at table with his disciples,
they thought they were the hosts and he the guest.
But then he broke the bread, and their eyes were opened
and they recognized him.
The guest became the host;
the foolish one was revealed as Wisdom.

To this table, to this banquet of Wisdom,
he calls us again.

GREAT PRAYER OF THANKSGIVING

The Lord be with you.
And also with you.
Lift up your hearts.
We lift them to the Lord.
Let us give thanks to the Lord our God.
It is right to give our thanks and praise.
It is right and our great delight to praise you, O God.
In the beginning of time, your wisdom danced through creation,
calling forth light and life.
Through wisdom, you formed us in your image,
calling us to love and serve you.
Foolishly we turned from you
and abandoned your ways of justice and mercy.
Yet you did not reject us,
but continued to call us and claim us as your own.

We were slaves in Egypt, and you freed us.
We were hungry and thirsty in the wilderness,
and you nourished us with manna and water from the rock.
We had no home, and you led us into the land of your promise.
We worshiped idols of our own making,
and you called to us through the prophets to turn back to you.
At last you emptied yourself of power
and came to us as the child of Mary,
holy God in frail and human flesh.

Therefore we praise you,
joining our voices with choirs of angels
and with all the faithful of every time and place,
who forever sing to the glory of your name:
Holy, holy, holy Lord, God of power and might,
heaven and earth are full of your glory.
Hosanna in the highest!
Blessed is he who comes in the name of the Lord.
Hosanna in the highest!

You are holy, O God of power and might,
and blessed is Jesus Christ, the one who comes in your name.
In his life, he called unlikely people to follow him:

fisherfolk, tax collectors, children,
sinners, deniers, betrayers.
On the cross he gave himself up to the powers of this world,
showing in his body your great foolishness, O God,
for loving such a wayward world.
Yet by this very cross, O Wisdom from on high,
you have undone and remade the wisdom of this world,
drawing light from darkness, power from humiliation,
life from death itself.

Remembering your gracious acts in Jesus Christ,
we proclaim together the mystery of faith:
Christ has died, Christ is risen, Christ will come again.

Come, then, life-giving Spirit,
brood over these bodily things
and make us into one body with Christ,
that we, who are baptized into his death,
may walk in newness of life;
that what is sown in dishonor may be raised in glory
and what is sown in weakness may be raised in power.

We praise you, O God,
blessed and holy Trinity,
now and forever. **Amen.**

ALL SAINTS

The Lord be with you.
And also with you.
Lift up your hearts.
We lift them to the Lord.
Let us give thanks to the Lord our God.
It is right to give our thanks and praise.

With Isaiah the prophet, we give you thanks—
for the promise of your heavenly banquet,
a feast of rich food and well-aged wine;
for the strength of your steadfast love,
destroying the shroud of sin and shame;
for the gift of your saving grace,
our long-awaited day of deliverance.

Therefore we rejoice in you,
singing with the saints of every age:
Holy, holy, holy Lord, God of power and might,
heaven and earth are full of your glory.
Hosanna in the highest.
Blessed is he who comes in the name of the Lord.
Hosanna in the highest.

With Mary and Martha, we remember Jesus—
his liberating word and healing touch,
his saving death and life-giving resurrection,
his promised return and glorious realm.

With thanksgiving, we remember
how Jesus took the bread, blessed and broke it,
and gave it to his disciples, saying:
This is my body, given for you.
Do this in remembrance of me.

We remember how he took the cup, saying:
This cup is the new covenant in my blood.
Do this in remembrance of me.

As often as we share this bread and cup,
we proclaim the saving death of the living Lord,
until he comes in glory to reign.

Praise to you, Lord Jesus:
Dying you destroyed our death,
rising you restored our life.
Lord Jesus, come in glory.

Pour out your Holy Spirit upon us, O God,
as we share this feast of bread and wine.
Make us one in the body of Christ our Lord
and one in the company of your saints.

With John the Divine, we look with hope—
for the coming of your new creation,
a new heaven and a new earth;
for an end to suffering and mourning,
when every tear will be wiped away;
for the fulfillment of your ancient promise
on the day when you make all things new.

Through Christ, the Alpha and Omega,
in the communion of the Holy Spirit,
all glory and honor are yours, O God,
now and forever. **Amen.**

REIGN OF CHRIST

God be with you.
And also with you.
Lift up your hearts.
We lift them to God.
Let us give thanks to the Lord our God.
It is right to give our thanks and praise.

Blessing, honor, and glory are yours, O God,
eternal source of all creation.
You are mightier than the thunder of waters,   *Ps. 93:4*
mightier than the waves of the sea.
You are majesty on high.

Yet when the time was right
you sent your Son,
a vulnerable infant of low estate,
to testify to the truth of power
made known in your embracing love.

Jesus came to raise up the poor
and cast down the mighty.
He taught us, like no other,
that your kingdom is one of forgiveness,
where human needs are daily met
and we are set free for love.

To you be glory and dominion forever.   *Dan. 7:14; Rev. 1:6*

And so we praise you as we say:
Holy, holy, holy Lord,
God of power and love,
heaven and earth are full of your glory.
Hosanna in the highest.
Blessed is the One who comes in the name of the Lord.
Hosanna in the highest.

On the night before he died for us
Jesus gathered his friends for a meal.
He took bread, gave you thanks, broke it,
gave it to them, and said:
Take, eat, this is my body
which is given for you;
do this in remembrance of me.

After supper he took the cup;
when he had given thanks,
he gave it to them and said:
This cup is the new covenant in my blood
poured out for the forgiveness of sins;
do this in remembrance of me.

Christ has died,
Christ has risen,
Christ will come in glory.

Remembering all that he has done for us,
his life, death, and resurrection,
we offer you our praise and thanks.
Send your Holy Spirit upon our celebration, and us,
that we may be fed with the body and blood of your Son
and be filled with your life-giving Spirit.

Unite us in Christ and one to another
from every tribe, people, language, and nation
to reveal your justice in the world,
and crown us with your holy wisdom
that we may we never lose sight of your reign of peace.

All this we ask through your Son,
Jesus Christ our Savior,
who with you and the Holy Spirit
reigns in glory,
now and forever. **Amen.**

Scripture Index

OLD TESTAMENT

Genesis 2:18–24	195
Genesis 3:8–15	25
Exodus 16:2–4, 9–15	108
Numbers 11:4–6, 10–16, 24–29	186
Deuteronomy 4:1–2, 6–9	146
Deuteronomy 5:12–15	14
Deuteronomy 6:1–9	229
Joshua 24:1–2a, 14–18	136
Ruth 1:1–18	225
Ruth 3:1–5; 4:13–17	238
1 Samuel 1:4–20	246
1 Samuel 2:1–10	246
1 Samuel 3:1–10 (11–20)	10
1 Samuel 7:(1a, 4–11, 19–23) 32–49	42
1 Samuel 8:4–11 (12–15), 16–20 (11:14–15)	21
1 Samuel 15:34–16:13	31
1 Samuel 17:57–18:5, 10–16	42
2 Samuel 1:1, 17–27	53
2 Samuel 5:1–5, 9–10	62
2 Samuel 6:1–5, 12b–19	71
2 Samuel 7:1–14a	81
2 Samuel 11:1–15	91
2 Samuel 11:26–12:13a	102
2 Samuel 18:5–9, 15, 31–33	112
2 Samuel 23:1–7	254
1 Kings 2:10–12; 3:3–14	122
1 Kings 8:(1, 6, 10–11) 22–30, 41–43	131
1 Kings 17:8–16	242
1 Kings 19:4–8	117
2 Kings 4:42–44	97
Esther 7:1–6, 9–10; 9:20–22	181
Job 1:1; 2:1–10	190
Job 23:1–9, 16–17	199
Job 38:1–7 (34–41)	208
Job 38:1–11	47
Job 42:1–6, 10–17	216
Psalm 1	172
Psalm 8	195
Psalm 9:9–20	42
Psalm 14	91
Psalm 15	146
Psalm 16	250
Psalm 19	161
Psalm 19:7–14	186
Psalm 20	31
Psalm 22:1–15	199
Psalm 23	87
Psalm 24	71, 233
Psalm 26	190
Psalm 29	1
Psalm 30	58
Psalm 34:1–8	117
Psalm 34:1–8 (19–22)	216
Psalm 34:9–14	127
Psalm 34:15–22	136
Psalm 45:1–2, 6–9	141
Psalm 48	62
Psalm 51:1–12	102
Psalm 54	177
Psalm 78:23–29	108
Psalm 81:1–10	14
Psalm 84	131
Psalm 85:8–13	77
Psalm 89:20–37	81
Psalm 90:12–17	204
Psalm 91:9–16	212
Psalm 92:1–4, 12–15	36
Psalm 93	259
Psalm 103:1–13, 22	5
Psalm 104:1–9, 24, 35c	208
Psalm 107:1–3, 23–32	47
Psalm 111	122
Psalm 116:1–9	166

Psalm 119:1–8	229	Mark 6:30–34, 53–56	81, 87
Psalm 123	67	Mark 7:1–8, 14–15,	
Psalm 124	181	21–23	141, 146
Psalm 125	151	Mark 7:24–37	151, 156
Psalm 126	220	Mark 8:27–38	161, 166
Psalm 127	238	Mark 9:30–37	172, 177
Psalm 130	25, 53,	Mark 9:38–50	181, 186
	112	Mark 10:2–16	190, 195
Psalm 132:1–12 (13–18)	254	Mark 10:17–31	199, 204
Psalm 133	42	Mark 10:35–45	208, 212
Psalm 138	21	Mark 10:46–52	216, 220
Psalm 139:1–6, 13–18	10	Mark 12:28–34	225, 229
Psalm 145:10–18	97	Mark 12:38–44	238, 242
Psalm 146	156, 225,	Mark 13:1–8	246, 250
	242	John 3:1–17	1
Proverbs 1:20–33	161	John 6:1–21	91, 97
Proverbs 9:1–6	127	John 6:24–35	102, 108
Proverbs 22:1–2, 8–9, 22–23	151	John 6:35, 41–51	112, 117
Proverbs 31:10–31	172	John 6:51–58	122, 127
Song of Solomon 2:8–13	141	John 6:56–69	131, 136
Isaiah 6:1–8	1	John 11:32–44	233
Isaiah 25:6–9	233	John 18:33–37	254, 259
Isaiah 35:4–7a	156	Romans 8:12–17	1
Isaiah 50:4–9a	166	2 Corinthians 3:1–6	5
Isaiah 53:4–12	212	2 Corinthians 4:5–12	10, 14
Jeremiah 11:18–20	177	2 Corinthians 4:13–5:1	21, 25
Jeremiah 23:1–6	87	2 Corinthians 5:6–10	
Jeremiah 31:7–9	220	(11–13), 14–17	31, 36
Lamentations 3:22–33	58	2 Corinthians 6:1–13	42, 47
Ezekiel 2:1–5	67	2 Corinthians 8:7–15	53, 58
Ezekiel 17:22–24	36	2 Corinthians 12:2–10	62, 67
Daniel 7:9–10, 13–14	259	Ephesians 1:3–14	71, 77
Daniel 12:1–3	250	Ephesians 2:11–22	81, 87
Hosea 2:14–20	5	Ephesians 3:14–21	91, 97
Amos 5:6–7, 10–15	204	Ephesians 4:1–16	102, 108
Amos 7:7–15	77	Ephesians 4:25–5:2	112, 117
		Ephesians 5:15–20	122, 127
NEW TESTAMENT		Ephesians 6:10–20	131, 136
Mark 2:13–22	5	Hebrews 1:1–4; 2:5–12	190, 195
Mark 2:23–3:6	10, 14	Hebrews 4:12–16	199, 204
Mark 3:20–35	21, 25	Hebrews 5:1–10	208, 212
Mark 4:26–34	31, 36	Hebrews 7:23–28	216, 220
Mark 4:35–41	42, 47	Hebrews 9:11–14	225, 229
Mark 5:21–43	53, 58	Hebrews 9:24–28	238, 242
Mark 6:1–13	62, 67	Hebrews 10:11–14 (15–18),	
Mark 6:14–29	71, 77	19–25	246, 250

James 1:17–27   141, 146
James 2:1–10 (11–13),
    14–17   151, 156
James 3:1–12   161, 166
James 3:13–4:3, 7–8a   172, 177
James 5:13–20   181, 186
Revelation 1:4b–8   254, 259
Revelation 21:1–6a   233

APOCRYPHA
Wisdom of Solomon
    1:13–15; 2:23–24   58
Wisdom of Solomon
    1:16–2:1, 12–22   177
Wisdom of Solomon
    3:1–9   233
Wisdom of Solomon
    7:26–8:1   166